Advance Praise for

"This is no ordinary book—it's the Swiss Army knife of communication—a set of tools to build strong relationships and avoid communication breakdowns. *Smart Talk* is fun to read, based on sound theory, and includes inspirational examples. Carry out the suggested chapter challenges and you'll soon solve communication problems at work and in your private life."

—Mary M. Mitchell, etiquette expert, syndicated columnist, and author of *The Complete Idiot's Guide to Modern Manners*

"Lisa is a dynamic and engaging public speaker, and this book shows you how to be an amazing communicator as well. No business person or educator should be without *Smart Talk*. Deep and wide, yet beautifully simple, it's a fantastic read. Should be required reading for every graduating student."

—Garr Reynolds, author of *Presentation Zen* and *The Naked Presenter*

"Lisa Marshall's book gives you a tool kit to get results. One of the most painful things I've witnessed is watching people who want to introduce themselves but are held back by their own doubts, by their own perceived lack of personality or anything interesting to say. This is the book I'd like to glue on a stick and hit them over the head with."

—Christopher S. Penn, digital marketing executive, bestselling author, and actual ninja

"A smart resource for real-life scenarios, *Smart Talk* teaches you easy ways to have confidence and conviction behind your words."

—Tracy Davidson, anchor/consumer watch reporter NBC10 News Philadelphia

"*Smart Talk* is a powerful, practical book that every manager needs. From giving feedback, to delivering bad news and dealing with difficult people, to influence and negotiation, it covers all the areas you need to communicate effectively and to navigate communication breakdowns. Best of all, it's easy to read and you can apply the techniques instantly."

—Dr. Nina Aversano, professor of management and
organizational behavior, director of the MBA program at the
College of Mount Saint Vincent

"Lisa has written an honest and helpful guide that teaches us all how to be more approachable and successful in every human interaction we experience. Anyone who reads this book will leave with a renewed sense of adventure and at least one new trick to try out. This book is a great teacher."

—C. C. Chapman, author of *Amazing Things Will Happen*

"No matter if you're a millionaire or recent graduate, *Smart Talk* gives you the edge. This handy reference guide distills the most recent research in business communication and makes it available to you in an easy-to-read format. With *Smart Talk* you'll learn the best techniques to achieve the results you want. Simple, yet so powerful, practical, and effective."

—Jaime Tardy, creator and host of *Eventual Millionaire*

"Whether you're a C-level executive or a recent graduate, *Smart Talk* is for you. This handy reference covers how to give feedback, accept criticism, deal with difficult people, and many other common professional challenges. Put Lisa's advice into action and you'll be more successful."

—Keitha Kinne, CFA, CAIA, CIMA,
chief operating officer at Managers Investment Group

"Lisa B. Marshall writes in a style that is conversational, fun to read, and helpful for novice and experienced communicators alike. This book takes the best of her podcasts and consolidates them into an easy-to-follow skill-building guide. This is the book I highly recommend to those who are seeking to become effective communicators and smarter talkers!"

—Laura Dean Mooney, motivational speaker and former president/ spokesperson for Mothers Against Drunk Driving

"*Smart Talk* is the perfect reference guide for time-starved small business owners. It provides the latest best practices and ideas for communicating effectively with your target customers and employees. Get this must-have resource to become a better business leader."

—Melinda F. Emerson, aka SmallBizLady, CEO of Quintessence Multimedia, *Forbes* #1 Woman for Entrepreneurs to follow on Twitter, and author of *Become Your Own Boss in 12 Months*

"Practical and engaging, *Smart Talk* is a book that will make a difference in your career and your life. Learn how to communicate effectively in every situation from making conversation, to dealing with conflict and difficult people, to influencing others. These skills are a missing foundation piece of our education system."

—David J. Lieberman, Ph.D., bestselling author of *Get Anyone to Do Anything* and *Never Be Lied to Again*

"The most valuable people in business and life are those who can effectively communicate ideas that move others to action. In *Smart Talk*, Lisa B. Marshall nails it head on. If you want to unleash your true potential, read this book!"

—Jeb Blount, CEO of SalesGravy.com and author of *People Buy You: The Real Secret to What Matters Most in Business*

"If you are looking for success that will take you to the moon, *Smart Talk* is the rocket ship that will get you there."

—Lee Tsao, managing partner at BizTech

SMART TALK

The Public Speaker's Guide
to Success in Every Situation

LISA B. MARSHALL

 ST. MARTIN'S GRIFFIN ❧ NEW YORK

www.stmartins.com

Design by Meryl Sussman Levavi

Library of Congress Cataloging-in-Publication Data

Marshall, Lisa B.
    Smart talk : the public speaker's guide to success in every situation / by Lisa B. Marshall.—First St. Martin's Griffin edition.
        pages cm
    Includes bibliographical references.
    ISBN 978-0-312-59728-3 (trade pbk.)
    ISBN 978-1-250-02958-4 (e-book)
    1. Public speaking.   I. Title.
    PN4129.15.M365 2013
    808.5'1—dc23

                                                                2012038338

First Edition: January 2013

10   9   8   7   6   5   4   3   2   1

Armando, Ariana, Daniela,
John, Mom, and Dad.

And to your success!

You're Invited!
Take the *Smart Talk* Success Quiz!

Are you *Smart Talk* successful?
Visit www.smarttalksuccess.com/quiz to learn your *Smart Talk* Success score. When you've finished the book, go back and take the quiz again. Compare your scores to measure how much you've learned!

Contents

Acknowledgments

Thanks first to my husband, Armando, and my children, Daniela and Ariana. I smile when I think of all the love and support I receive from you daily. Girls, I wrote this book for you so that you will know what I didn't know! You were my inspiration. Even if you are the only two people who read and benefit from this book, I'll know my efforts were worth it! I love you with all my heart.

I want to thank my two best friends who have supported me throughout my life: Linda Remington and Larissa Whitman. It is a rarity to have friends like you and I am privileged to have you in my life.

The ones who made everything possible were Grammar Girl (aka Mignon Fogarty) and the rest of the Quick and Dirty Tips team at Macmillan. I'd like to especially thank Beata Santora for her excellent editing. This book is so much better because of you. Thanks!

Thanks to my professors who helped me to complete my master's degree in organizational and interpersonal communication: Donald Cushman, Michael Huspek, and Sara Cobb.

Thanks to my clients who trusted me and urged me to expand my programs over the years.

Thanks to the Lisa B. Marshall support team: Lou Crocetto, Sherri Barksdale, Michelle O'Shea, Tim Roufa, Whitney Punchak, and Mallory Rhodes. I appreciate all of your contributions.

I'd like to thank the "beta readers" for their insights, recommendations, and encouragement: Linda Remington, Ken Flowe, Deborah Spivack, Christopher Incao, Bill Jackman, Glen Munro, Tatenda Mupini, Cristopher G. Johnson, Brian Schardt, Bill Jackman, Alison Scheid, Sarmi Gilani, Reeteka Sud, Taha Arbaoui, Cindy Labaz, Reece Sellin, Fernando Marono, Bonnie Wong, Whitney Bishop, Mr. & Mrs. Laura Baboolal, and Stephanie Kiernan.

Without the support of *The Public Speaker* community, this book wouldn't have been possible. Thanks to all the listeners, readers, and fans of *The Public Speaker* podcast who have supported me, especially Marie-Adele Guicharnaud, Piper Hendricks, Syed Quadri, Chris Woodhouse, Dan Murrell, Brian Mattocks, Bob Levy, Terry D. Kozlyk, Jeff Hurt, Connie Malamed, Jeremy Goh, Kris Harty, and Artem Daniliants.

Special thanks to Dr. Robert Cialdini, Trisha Liu, Angela Lauria, Mac Smith, Kathleen Walker, David McGuire, Ali Brown, Barrett Peterson, Steve and Jennifer Chou, Rabbi Eli Adler, Dr. Ken Flowe, and Beth Beutler.

To my brothers and sisters: Deb Boehm-Davis, Ron Boehm, Rich Boehm, and Maria Watson; and to Grandma Vincenza and Grandma Ita. Love to you all.

I miss you, Mom, Dad, and John.

SMART
TALK

Introduction:
The (Not So) Hidden Cost of
Saying the Wrong Thing

You teach best what you most need to learn.

—RICHARD BACH, *ILLUSIONS: THE ADVENTURES OF A RELUCTANT MESSIAH*

Have you ever been surprised to find out you weren't as good or as smart as you thought? I'll always remember the day I was called into Bob Goodman's office. He was a very senior manager and I was just a young management trainee at General Electric. I could feel my stomach doing flip-flops as I apprehensively entered his office. After some small talk he told me something I have *never* forgotten. He said:

> "Lisa, you are like a big ship, like a cruise liner, coming into port. You rock all of the other small ships and you don't even realize it. We'd like to help you with that. We want to send you to some training."

It turns out GE wanted to send me to a training course to improve my interpersonal communication skills. I was mortified!

Obviously, at that time, I didn't know what I didn't know.

We're taught reading and writing in school, yet rarely (if ever), are we taught to be smart about what we say and how we say it. We aren't taught *communication* skills.

For example:

- Do you know specific methods of introducing yourself that will form positive first impressions and lead to strong relationships (and the ways an introduction can limit your chances of ever building a relationship)?
- Do you know all the specific ways to shake hands that instill confidence and trustworthiness (and the common mistakes that many people make)?
- Do you know how to move beyond initial conversations? Beyond collecting friends or fans, to sincerely and effectively engage with people and create significant, meaningful relationships?
- Do you know what to say when someone is going through a difficult time?
- Do you know how to deliver effective feedback without using the old "sandwich approach"—which, by the way, doesn't work?
- Do you know how to respond to criticism?
- Do you know alternative ways to say "no" yet still develop and build a relationship?
- Do you know how to respond with diplomacy, tact, and grace?
- Do you know how to deliver difficult news or how to handle a difficult conversation?
- Do you know what to say when dealing with a bully, a whiner, or any other difficult person?
- Do you know what makes a master negotiator different from a novice negotiator?
- Do you know what to say to effectively persuade and influence others?
- Do you know how our brains are wired to cause attraction, likability, and trustworthiness?

Too often, the answer to all of these questions is "no." Or worse, we have some vague notions that trick us into thinking that we know the answers. And we realize that we really don't know what to say only when we have a problem . . . *after* we've significantly damaged a relationship.

That leads me to the rest of my story . . .

The man sitting next to me at the communication skills training seemed very unhappy—a curmudgeon. He explained that he worked for the post office and that every year there is a communication skills survey among the employees and the managers who score the lowest are forced to come to this course. "Charm school" he called it.

At the training, our first task was to take an inventory of our communication style, adding up points for different measures. After hearing his story, I couldn't help myself. I was dying to see the scores for this rough-edged guy from the post office, so I peeked over to see his scores.

What I noticed immediately was that our scores for each and every category *were exactly the same!* (I even double-checked and triple checked his scores against mine. It's a moment in my life I've never forgotten.)

I was stunned.

It was then that I realized I needed to change. I promised myself that I would commit myself to practicing and improving my communication skills. I promised that I would polish my people skills. I promised that I would learn as much as I could to become smart about communication. That was just the very beginning of my journey.

I learned a lot in the next twenty-five years.

Finding My Passion

After finishing the initial two-year management training program at GE, I was asked to join GE's corporate audit staff, an accelerated leadership development program. That was when I first noticed that the root cause of many organization issues stemmed from problems in communication. (Interestingly, much later, in 2009, I read a small study[1] that reported that the cost of poor communication was approximately $35,500 *per worker* per year.)

Fortunately, at the time, GE recognized the importance of communication and encouraged me to get a master's degree in organizational and interpersonal communication to bring that knowledge into the organization. (They even paid for it. Thanks, GE!)

On the personal side of things, this was also about the time that I met John. He was the kind of person who naturally attracts other people, like a magnet. His passion and enthusiasm for life was contagious. Unfortunately, he was terminally ill. He was dying from a horrible disease, yet he was the most alive person that I have ever met. That's why I eventually married him.

During my years with John, I gained a different kind of education in communication. John had AIDS in the late 1980s, a time when there was significant social stigma associated with people who were HIV positive. Even medical staff were often extremely insensitive. That's when I first became painfully aware of the communication issues within the health-care industry. Of course, very personally, I was also learning how to deal with difficult and emotionally charged interpersonal communication.

Who I Am Now

It's been many years since then and I've dedicated my professional life to helping individuals and organizations improve productivity by building and enhancing communication skills. I've developed and delivered hundreds of communication workshops, keynotes, and seminars in areas such as teambuilding, public speaking, networking, conflict, and leadership, both as a corporate employee and as an independent communication strategist.

In 2008, I wanted to expand my reach to help more people than just the ones who came to hear me speak. So I created *The Public Speaker's Quick and Dirty Tips for Improving Your Communication*

Skills, a free weekly podcast on the Quick and Dirty Tips network. The episodes have been downloaded more than eight million times in over 200 countries. In 2009, the show was nominated as a top five business podcast by the Podcast Awards and a year later it was also nominated in the education category. (Yay!) In 2012, I partnered with Hewlett-Packard to offer a free daily, bite-sized communication-building briefing[2] called *Communication Success: Tips For Busy People,* that is delivered directly to printers worldwide! I'm very excited because for the first time, my work is available in several languages.

My goal with all of my programs is to provide proven, evidence-based strategies and practical techniques that have an immediate impact in your organization, in your career, and in your life. I want to help you have the competitive edge to get things done, big and small. I want you to be a master of communication. I'd like to help you be more:

- Confident—so you are comfortable in your own skin and accepting of others
- Passionate—so you live life based on what's important to you
- Sensitive—so you can easily tap into your emotions and the emotions of others
- Consistent—so you constantly demonstrate how much you value your relationships
- Persistent—so you keep communicating even with obstacles in your way
- Energetic—so you create and attract positive energy
- Diplomatic—so you always consider the perspective of others
- Visionary—so you know exactly what you want and how to share your vision with others
- Positive—so you always focus on the positive and expect good outcomes
- Successful—so you achieve your goals, financial or otherwise, while creating, developing, and growing strong relationships

I believe a true master communicator, a *smart talker,* is able to demonstrate *all* of these abilities in every interaction. And if you are able to become a true master of communication, either as an individual, as a team, or as an organization, then you're unstoppable!

That's why I wrote this book. What's been missing from the shelves of your bookstore (or the files on your e-reader) is a communication reference resource, a guide that takes up-to-date communication research and applies it to practical, everyday situations that we all face, and gives smart, step-by-step directions on how to achieve results and success.

Think of this book as your Swiss Army knife of communication!

Smart Talk is a handy, no-nonsense, skill-building guide for both tongue-tied novices and advanced communicators who have found themselves in hot water (or who want to keep themselves out of it!).

As you read the book, make sure you also take the quizzes and chapter challenges.

Really take them.

I'd like for you to do more than just read about interesting ideas and techniques. My goal is for you to gain new skills and enhance your current communication abilities. After all, you can't learn to swim from reading a book, you need to jump into the pool and practice. While you are reading each chapter, apply the new information to your own life.

By thinking through the quiz questions and trying the challenges, you will help your brain to form new communication patterns. The chapter quizzes help you to become aware of your current communication skills and the challenges help you to put into action the new strategies and techniques you've learned. For those who want even more, I've created a free members-only VIP Web site. If you choose to register, you'll get exclusive access to additional resources, interviews, and opportunities to interact directly with me.

VIP Bonus: To see all of the bonus VIP content, join now at www.smarttalksuccess.com/VIP. Or you can simply discover these exclusive bonuses throughout the book wherever you see this symbol:

Use the case studies at the end of each chapter for inspiration. Perhaps most important, I strongly urge you to keep practicing.

Keep a copy of this book close by at home and at work and when faced with a communication challenge. Use it as your reference guide to refresh or expand your skills, to be a *smart talker.*

I wanted to share my story with you partly as an introduction, partly as a confession, and hopefully, partly as motivation for those who struggle mastering these crucial people skills. My tag line for my business has always been, "I'm passionate about communication. Your success is my business."

I hope you now understand that it's not just a tag line, it's really what I believe in.

1. Taking the "Hell" Out of Hello: How to Introduce Yourself

Please allow me to introduce myself / I'm a man of wealth and taste / I've been around for a long, long year / Stole many a man's soul and faith.

—THE ROLLING STONES, "SYMPATHY FOR THE DEVIL"

When I was a young General Electric (GE) management trainee, I attended quarterly status meetings. One time we were waiting over thirty minutes for senior managers to arrive. As my luck would have it, nature was calling, so I left to use the restroom. On my way back, I was in a hurry and literally ran into someone in the hallway.

When I looked up, I immediately realized I had just bumped into Jack Welch, then CEO of GE. Of course, I was embarrassed and started apologizing. He smiled, stuck out his hand to shake, and said, "Well, hello, I'm Jack Welch." I laughed and said, "Yes, of course, you are—I know who you are." He responded very graciously, by saying, "And you are?"

As a very young eager management trainee this was my perfect opportunity to introduce myself and make a great first impression.

But I wasn't prepared. I really wasn't sure what to say, so I stammered. When I returned to my seat I could still feel the heat in my face. I was so embarrassed and angry at myself because I had delivered such a poor self-introduction and had blown an opportunity to make a great first impression.

Although most of us don't meet a well-known and influential CEO like Jack Welch every day, we do meet scores of people in our daily life—at our jobs, at parties, at networking events, or even in the supermarket check-out line. And it's impossible to know ahead of time when you might meet someone who could have a big impact on your life.

 Quick Quiz: Think about the last time you introduced yourself. Who was it? How did it go? Do you remember what you said? What opportunities have you gained because you took the risk and introduced yourself to a stranger?

First impressions are critically important. We size each other up very quickly. One study[1] suggests that we unconsciously comprehend what something is and decide whether we like it or not in as little as 1/10 of a second. Another study showed[2] that first impressions as short as three minutes play a major role in determining the course of a relationship. Even when we're presented with lots of evidence to the contrary, we're attached to our initial impressions of people. This is why creating a positive first impression is so crucial.

In essence, our introductory behaviors and words are what we use to gauge if we want to take a next step with that person. Specifically, an introduction is used to evaluate if you can help your conversation partner, or if he or she can help you.

Ultimately, a good introduction is a short, focused statement or question that is interesting to your listener—with the latter being the most important. That is the purpose of any introduction, to gain the interest of your conversation partner so the initial connection can advance to conversation-making and building rapport.

Early on in my career, I was fearful to introduce myself to people I perceived as "above me" in rank. I also thought that in general, small talk was useless (I used to call it *plastic talk*) because it seemed so fake and artificial. So I avoided introducing myself and making conversations.

Although I did network internally, I didn't do it nearly enough or with the right mix of people. I didn't network externally at all. My career suffered. Because I didn't have strong connections, many times my intentions were misunderstood, or worse, colleagues thought I was purposefully being disrespectful.

After some coaching, I finally understood that introduction and small talk were just a way to begin to move toward meaningful conversations and that networking effectively was critically important to career success. My coach said to me, "Lisa, you don't ask someone to marry you on the first date! You need to warm-up first." That made sense! Before I can ask someone important questions, I first needed the person to respond favorably to me, to like me, and perhaps most important, to trust me. It was like a huge lightbulb went off in my head—introductions, small talk, and initial conversations are just a first step toward genuine communication.

 Check This Out: Visit www.smarttalksuccess.com /extras to see a very funny (but fake) eHarmony introduction. It's a great example of what *not* to do.

The Best Self-Introduction I've Ever Received

Oddly, the best self-introduction that I've ever received was not a professional one. It was a letter. Prior to the start of their kindergarten year, my children each received a hand-written note from the school principal. She introduced herself by listing her favorite things to eat (pizza and popcorn) and by sharing her favorite summertime activities (going to the movies and to the beach).

My husband and I also received a letter of introduction. However, in our letter, the principal described her professional experience and educational background along with her goals for the school and for the children in the upcoming year.

My children and I immediately liked the principal because she shared things about herself that overlapped with our own interests. She successfully created a strong first impression, which engendered a positive reaction in us.

A well-crafted, strong self-introduction is a critical part of making a good first impression. It's no wonder that "how to make an introduction" is one of the most commonly searched topics on *The Public Speaker* blog, and the most commonly asked question I receive during networking workshops.

 Quick Quiz: Before you read the steps to an effective introduction, take a shot at introducing yourself to someone. It could be to me, to a friend, or to anyone. You'll want to keep this one as your "before" so you can compare your progress after reading the steps.

Now, that you've given it a try, here are the five steps to effective introductions. Skipping these five basics may cost you the opportunity of a lifetime.

Step #1: Make It Relevant to Your Audience

The most important part of any introduction is to consider your audience. Who exactly are you introducing yourself to? What will they find interesting and compelling? What can you share that might help you make a connection and quickly build common ground?

When I teach introductions and conversation-making in workshops, I tell the participants to think of themselves as a series of ever-larger concentric circles. At the center is your heart. What you keep deep in your heart is highly personal; things that perhaps you only share with yourself or maybe your partner. As you move out from there, you have your emotions, your values, and your culture, moving further out your interests and activities, your roles, your experiences, and your immediate environment.

When we enter a roomful of strangers, we're all separate circles scattered throughout the room.

When we introduce ourselves, our outer circles begin to touch. With time, as we move from introduction to conversation, our circles begin to overlap. The overlap is how we build rapport.

The process of introduction starts with a smile, direct eye contact, and good posture. You need to walk and stand with assurance. These nonverbal behaviors are powerful and communicate confidence, trust, and sincerity. They make you more attractive, approachable, and memorable.

Check This Out: Introductions can be serious, funny, artistic, and specific. Visit www.smarttalksuccess.com /extras to see three very different (and creative) introduction videos.

Step #2: Shake Hands

The next step is to shake hands. Cold fish are expected at sushi bars and sweaty palms are fine at middle school dances. Neither screams professionalism. Know how to present a good handshake. A good handshake instills confidence, trustworthiness, and can make or break a deal. Most important, it leaves a lasting impression.

Quick Quiz: Think about how and when you shake hands. Have you ever made an instant decision/perception (positive or negative) about anyone based purely on his or her handshake?

To shake, reach forward with your right hand, keeping your elbow in and slightly flexed. Keep your drink or objects in your left hand, so that only your right is available for shaking (make sure it's not cold and wet).

Your right hand should be open, your palm perpendicular to the floor and your thumb pointing upward. Be sure to fully expose the web of your hand (that's the fleshy part between your index finger and thumb.)

It's critically important that the web of your hand touch the web of the other person's hand, first, before your fingers wrap around. Then, and only then, firmly squeeze. In fact, this initial web-to-web contact is the key to a successful handshake.

Research[3] suggests, that to be perceived as open and extroverted, you need to squeeze firmly. The strength of the grip should be strong enough so that you're applying and feeling a comfortable pressure, as when you hold a hammer or umbrella in one hand. To end the shake, pump once or twice and disconnect. You don't want to linger too long. Once you feel the grip of the other person loosen, you should let go, even if you are still talking.

Finally, it's always good to make a habit of observing handshake subtleties. We typically shake both before and after a meeting. You'll want to notice if there are any differences between the first and second shakes. Did the second one last a bit longer? Did the person stand a little closer to you? Did the other party smile more at you? These are all indicators that the meeting may have gone well.

 Warning: Greetings and handshakes vary around the world. For example, in Japan, the customary greeting is a bow, or a weak handshake. Research[4] customs surrounding handshakes when you are participating in another culture.

Step #3: Say the Other Person's Name While Shaking

If possible, when introducing yourself start with the name of the *other* person. Of course, in a letter or online, that's easy to do: "Dear Mr. Incao" or "Hi, Chris." In person, it's tempting to start with your own name, but if you know the name of the other person, use his name first. In a group setting, you can just say "Hi, everyone!"

This brings me to a fine point. Do you use a person's last name or first name? In the United States, it's common to greet people by first names, unless the person is significantly above you in rank. However, in many other cultures, it is much more common to greet someone more formally—as in Ms. Winslet or Mr. Chairman. If you're not sure, go with the more formal approach and the person you're greeting will likely let you know. When people call me Ms. Marshall, I always respond by saying, "Please, call me Lisa."

Once you've said your greeting, then you should say your name. In fact, in a professional setting, it's important to say your name twice. It's also a good habit to s-l-o-w d-o-w-n c-o-n-s-i-d-e-r-a-b-l-y and say your name very clearly. In personal settings you might just say, "Hi, Mary Beth, I'm Lisa."

If it's a professional self-introduction, it's likely to be a bit more formal, "Hello, Mr. Jones, I'm Lisa, Lisa B. Marshall." Depending on the setting, you may also want to include your title, the company you work for, or other appropriate context information. When I accidentally bumped into Jack Welch, this is what I *should* have started with:

"Hello, Mr. Welch, I'm Lisa, Lisa Boehm [I was still single then]. I'm a graduate of the Information Systems Management Program and I am in my first year on the Corporate Audit Staff."

If you want to remember the other person's name, you may want to try to say the name of the other person twice during the introduction. That will help you to remember and it shows a genuine interest. Be aware, however, some people may feel like you're overdoing it by repeating his or her name more than once, so if you prefer, you can repeat the name silently in your thoughts.

 Warning: Don't introduce yourself as your nickname. "I'm Ginni Rometty." It's better to say, "I'm Virginia Rometty, but please call me Ginni."

Step #4: Build Rapport by Finding Common Ground

In the letter the principal sent to my children she mentioned that she likes to eat pizza and popcorn and go to the beach in the summer. Of course, she chose these particular activities on purpose—what kid doesn't like pizza, popcorn, or going to the beach? Similarly, in the parent introduction letter, she shares her goals for the new students during the year—which, of course, are shared by any parent.

It's really no different in a crowded conference.

"Hi, Mary, I'm Lisa, Lisa Marshall. I'm curious, what's been the most valuable part of the conference for you?"

The idea is to then build on the response. How can you relate to what the other person found valuable? Is this something you value too? If so, tell a story that demonstrates that shared value. If not, then choose a story that demonstrates a similar value.

I've used this technique in response to the question, "What do you do?" Instead of directly answering the question, I respond by saying, "I'll tell you what I do, however, I'd love to hear what you do first." Then, the information shared can be used to adjust the way I describe what I do so that it is more relevant and interesting to the listener.

During initial introductions, business professionals share their interests, goals, activities, and roles because these are areas you'll likely have overlap with, particularly when attending a professional conference. Although a professional connection is very likely, keep in mind, the connection doesn't have to be business-related. It doesn't even have to be of great importance (e.g. the weather, the news, etc.), just one that creates commonality that you can build upon to move the conversation forward.

Google Someone to Discover Common Ground

If you know ahead of time who you plan to introduce yourself to, you should think about doing a little research first. For example, I wanted to meet Guy Kawasaki (one of the first Apple evangelists and author of numerous books, including *Enchantment, Art of the Start, Hindsights,* and others). So, I read a few of his books and his blog in an effort to learn where our "circles" might overlap.

For example, early in my research, I learned that he loves hockey. But the only connection I have to hockey is that I played *field* hockey in middle school. Then, I found out that he enjoys Robert Scoble, Queen Latifah, and Jenny Lawson—three people who I also respect and enjoy. However, I didn't stop there; my research was extensive. It turns out that Guy and I have many areas of common ground. When I met him, our conversation naturally led to communication topics I had read on his blog and heard in recorded interviews, and it was easy to expand on those ideas and concepts. My research preparation certainly paid off, because we were able to easily connect in an enjoyable conversation.

Isn't That Stalking?

At this point, I'd need to take a detour to answer a question that I often get after I mention these "research" strategies. Often, a participant in a workshop will raise their hand and say, "Isn't that a little creepy or stalker-like?"

My response is: Well, that depends. Always let the context of the information and the situation guide you when choosing what to reveal from your research.

If someone has made information public by writing about it on a work-related blog or by leaving a comment in a forum or by including it in a book, it's fair game to bring it up. In fact, as long as your intention is to establish a professional connection, it's a good idea to bring it up, because it shows you are making an effort to get to know the person.

Sometimes, people will do that to me. They read something that I wrote several years ago, so it's fresh in their mind, and they will paraphrase or quote me, *to* me. I'll admit it feels a little odd, but at the same time it's flattering that someone has taken the time to read or listen to something I've written.

In Guy Kawasaki's book *Enchantment* he writes[5], "In my case, when strangers tell me they play hockey, they lower my resistance to their pitch because we have something in common. If nothing else, I respect them for making the effort to learn my passion."

Again, keep in mind the overall context of the conversation. Where did you gather the information? Why are you meeting this person? Is this a professional meeting or a personal one? Was the published information intended for the general public to consume? The context of the situation will dictate if your actions are "stalker-like" or not.

For example, in a professional setting you wouldn't suddenly veer off into personal information that you learned from a person's Facebook page. At the same time, if the same information was revealed on a blog, then go ahead and bring it up.

"Suzie, I noticed on your personal Facebook page that you like *Star Wars* movies. I do too."

Creepy.

"I noticed on your blog that you reference *Star Wars* movies a lot. I love those movies, too!"

Not creepy.

Finally, what do you do if you're not sure what the other's person passions are? Just start with "safe" topics (such as weather, sports, travel) and avoid anything controversial (like politics, ethics, religion).

Step #5: Communicate Confidence

An important part of any introduction is to communicate confidence. As you are saying your initial words and shaking hands, remember that the majority of your impact will actually come from your tone of voice and body language. You'll want to communicate enthusiasm by speaking slightly faster, smiling, making direct eye contact, and speaking with an upbeat, positive tone of voice.

Warning: Keep in mind that in most business settings your goal is to show confidence but not overconfidence. That might be perceived as intimidating and unappealing.

In some service professions, such as medical or legal providers, often the main purpose of an initial introduction is to instill confidence in you and your abilities. Again, the context of the situation warrants a different approach. In the case of a service provider introduction, instead of aiming to discover common ground, it's better to express something about your experience and credentials, perhaps along with a statement of concern. For example, if you were an emergency room patient which introduction would you prefer?

"Hi, I'm Dr. Flowe. I like hiking and the comedy of Jon Stewart." or

"Hi, I'm Dr. Flowe. I'll be your emergency doctor today. I've been doing this for sixteen years, and I'm Board Certified. My team and I will take great care of you today."

In a Roomful of People Focus on Two or Three Things Only

At times, a self-introduction may be one-sided—such as in a classroom when the students are asked to introduce themselves. In this case, you may be asked to provide specific information (like your name, occupation/major, and something unique about you), but at other times you may be free to respond in any manner you choose. The first case is easy—just remember to briefly include all of the requested details, and don't let the previous responses get you off track.

When the introduction details are your choice, I recommend picking three things (at most) that you think others in the group might relate to. This means you should *always* have six or seven sound bites prepared and in your mobile device. Sound bites are short messages that you are willing to share with strangers and that you've practiced. Ideally, this should be a mix of professional and personal items.

Think carefully about how you want to represent yourself. Again, the idea is to try to build rapport. By choosing just two or three things, your introduction will be more memorable. In addition, you can expand and contract the length of your response by providing examples or details for each of your chosen points.

For example, for a very short personal introduction I might say:

"Hi, everyone. I'm Lisa, Lisa Marshall. My girls are in second grade."

For a longer answer in a personal setting I might say:

"Hi, everyone. I'm Lisa. I'm a mother, author, and speaker. I enjoy dancing, although I'm not that good at it."

In a professional setting, I generally prefer to focus on three work-related things:

"Hi, everyone, I'm Lisa, Lisa B. Marshall. I'm a professional speaker, author, and podcast host."

For a longer professional answer, I might say:

"Hi, everyone, I'm Lisa, Lisa B. Marshall. I'm a professional speaker and author. I'm also known as The Public Speaker, because I am the host of a tips-based communication skills podcast called *The Public Speaker*. I'm excited because my second book, *Smart Talk*, just landed on the *New York Times* Bestseller list!" (A girl can dream, right?)

How to Introduce Yourself Via Telephone

Introducing yourself on the phone is a little bit different. I try to keep my self-introduction extremely short. I only share my name and one thing about me that the other person might know. For example: "Hello, Jen, I'm Lisa. My daughter is in Emily's class."

In a professional setting I'd say, "Hello Eli, I'm Lisa, Lisa Marshall. You might recognize my voice. I'm The Public Speaker." The idea is I don't want to spend too much time on me—I'm only interested in setting a context for the phone call.

If I am leaving a voice mail for someone I've never met before, at the very end of the message, I also usually add: "Oh, if you like, before you call me back, <smile> you can check me out at lisab marshall.com to get a better idea of who I am." (Yes, I do smile, even though it's a voice mail. The other person of course is not going to see my smile, but still you can hear a smile.)

One advantage of introducing yourself via telephone is that you can have notes in front of you. I would never suggest having complete paragraphs of information that you plan to share—instead, have a few phrases that will help you to remember what to include. This way, your message will sound conversational and not stiff.

How to Introduce Yourself Via E-mail or the Web

When I introduce myself via e-mail, I again prefer to keep it short with three main bullet points. I always include links so the person can learn more. That way if they are interested, they can click and if they are not, they can just keep reading. I might link to my Web site, or to *The Public Speaker* show, or to my LinkedIn profile, or to other online profiles that I maintain.

Again, I try to choose links that I think would be most relevant to the person I am introducing myself to. I usually try to offer something to the person, such as a free resource.

Web introductions are a mix of e-mail and telephone tips. Keep it short, but provide links to learn more. If you really want to engage the person, offer them something of value so that it isn't a one-sided exchange.

VIP Bonus: With the exponential growth of social media, often introductions are online rather than in-person. Download "The Best Social Media Introductions" and get other exclusive information and benefits by joining my free members-only VIP site by visiting www.smarttalksuccess .com/VIP.

The Smart Talk Un-Introduction

When introducing myself to a complete stranger, I prefer to be very brief and conversational. The idea behind an "un-introduction" is to ask an interesting question that helps lead your partner into a conversation and then later tell them who you are. In a social setting, it's easy. Just ask any open-ended question.

"What have you found most valuable/interesting/useful at the conference? . . . I'm Lisa, by the way."

"So, what do you do, when you're not doing this?"

In a professional setting (except perhaps in an interview setting, where it's usually best to let your interviewer lead the conversation) a really thoughtful question is often much more effective than anything you can say about yourself. That's why the un-introduction is my favorite approach.

I created the *Smart Talk* "un-introduction" technique based upon an exercise I read about in Jeffrey Gitomer's *Little Black Book of Connections*[6]. When you find yourself in a professional networking situation, Jeffrey suggests that you walk up to people based on the title on their name tag. He suggests that you say your name, and then ask a direct question. Here's how I've used his technique:

"Hi, I'm Lisa. Tell me, if you could magically fix the most significant communication issue in your organization overnight, how would tomorrow be different?"

Of course I've created and prepared follow-up questions, too:

"If you had to estimate, how much do you think poor communication costs your organization?"

"What have you tried to address your communication issues?"

"Do you have any plans in place now?"

The next step is where Jeffrey and I differ. In addition to a variety of follow-up questions, I also prepare and practice client stories. That way, when the person eventually asks me what I do (and they always do), I say "I'm a communication strategist and I help people like you. For example . . ." Then I'll I tell a client story about an organization I helped that had the same or similar problems as the person just described in response to my initial questions.

When I'm done telling the client story, I usually say, "You sound like you have an interesting and unique communication challenge. I'd love to learn more about the issues you're facing. Would you like to set up a time to discuss it in more detail? If I can help I'll certainly let you know, but if I can't, I'll help you find someone who can."

This approach takes some confidence, preparation, and practice to perfect. However, it can be highly efficient and an effective way to engage someone in a presales conversation and further your professional relationship.

Twenty-Five Years Later and I'm Still Working on How to Introduce Myself

At the end of "The Farmer in the Dell," I always feel sorry for the cheese. Everyone else—the farmer, the wife, the dog, the cat, the rat—all had someone or something to show for at the end of the day. The cheese, though, despite having an important farm-life role to play, finds itself at the end of exciting hi-ho-the-derry-o-ing, alone.

Don't make my mistake. Don't be the cheese.

I recently attended a conference for authors who wanted to become professional speakers. On the train returning home I realized I had made a big mistake. I didn't really connect with attendees as I usually do and it seemed to get worse as the conference went on. Looking back, I realized it had to do with how I was introducing myself. I failed to follow my own advice!

I introduced myself as a "professional speaker." You might be saying, "Well what's wrong with that? You *are* a professional speaker, aren't you?"

Yes, I am, but in this case saying that wasn't the best choice. I didn't keep in mind that the other attendees were there to learn how to become professional public speakers. A better and equally true answer could have been: "I am an author trying to make public speaking a bigger part of my business." Or "I'm a communication strategist trying to make public speaking a bigger part of my business."

The point is, my choice of words separated me from my fellow attendees. While I was unconsciously protecting my ego, I was creating distance. I am reluctant to admit this, but I also noticed that I chose not to introduce myself to some people based on the topic of their books. I won't lie, I was judging a person by his book (cover). If I thought the topic was "hocus-pocus," I didn't bother. That was a mistake. I lost business opportunities as a result.

Don't let this happen to you. It's the biggest connection mistake you can make. The challenge when making initial connections is to keep an open mind, to ask questions, and to listen.

 Warning: Even if your natural tendency is to spot the negatives in someone, always remind yourself that connecting is about finding common ground.

In his book, *Love Is the Killer App*, Tim Sanders advises[7]:

> Don't screen anyone out. Sometimes, those who may appear powerless or insignificant are potential stars, and someday they may become a key node in your network, and they will remember that you were on their side before they went large!

You just never know who you might meet and what impact they will have on your business or your life. Meeting someone can lead to nothing at all, or perhaps a small action step for you, or maybe it will change the direction of your business or your life.

I have provided you with my smart talk rules, guidelines and activities to help you introduce yourself. Now it's up to you to execute. Go, meet people! To help you get started, here are three *Smart Talk* chapter challenges.

Smart Talk Challenge #1
Introduce yourself to at least one stranger everyday for one week. Try introducing yourself in different ways each time. Make a game of it. (If you find introducing yourself difficult, start by simply smiling at strangers. For a more advanced challenge, choose settings that make you uncomfortable.)

Smart Talk Challenge #2
Find a Meet-Up group. Choose a group that's interesting to you and attend an event. Introduce yourself to as many people as you can. Make a game of it. The idea is to practice by introducing yourself differently each time. For a more advanced challenge, choose a group of people that you consider very different from you.

Smart Talk Challenge #3
Introduce yourself and meet other readers at www.smarttalksuc cess.com/intros. Oh go ahead, don't be shy! The more you practice the better your introductions will be. Besides, where else will you be able to get some feedback on your introduction and meet other readers of the same book. Pretty cool, huh?

Summary: How to Introduce Yourself

- ✓ The success or failure of your self-introduction impacts the success of the relationship and could have an impact on the rest of your life.
- ✓ Self-introductions are a critical part of first impressions. Not only are first impressions hard to change, they impact the progression of the relationship.
- ✓ To engage your conversation partner, your introduction must be relevant to them.
- ✓ The standard professional greeting is a firm, web-to-web handshake, with direct eye contact and good posture.
- ✓ The best introductions share common interests, goals, activities, and roles.

✓ Introductions demonstrate confidence but not overconfidence.
✓ For an introduction to a group, focus on an interest, a role, or an activity—perhaps two or three.
✓ On the telephone, very brief introductions are only to set the context of the call.
✓ For written Web introductions, include three short main points with links to details.
✓ Un-introductions start with a question, then lead to common ground.

Case Study: Allison P.

Allison approached me after a seminar once and told me that she had a very difficult time introducing herself and carrying on face-to-face conversations. She told me that often her in-person conversation partners seemed to quickly lose interest and, more important, didn't seem to take her seriously.

In fact, it was such a significant problem that it was hurting her during the job interview process. She was getting many telephone interviews, but not getting past her first in-person interviews.

I immediately saw the problem. She had difficultly maintaining any sort of eye contact during conversations. When she was talking with me, she was looking past me, up and to the right—as if she was looking at something that was beyond me. I explained to her that in our culture, eye contact is critical for creating a connection and when you can't hold someone's gaze, you are often perceived as untrustworthy. It was the lack of eye contact that was causing the misperceptions.

I showed her what she needed to do and we practiced for a few minutes right there at the event. I also gave her a few "homework" video exercises to do so she could improve.

About a year later, she came to see me again at a public workshop just to thank me. I could see the difference immediately. She enthusiastically told me that this one small change had made an incredible difference in both her professional and personal life. She told me that not only was she more comfortable with conversations, she had landed a great job, and she was surprised by how many people over the past year have commented on the difference they noticed in her "confidence" level.

🗨 🗨 🗨

I asked for listener/readers of my podcast to send me introductions. Here are some of the ones I particularly enjoyed:

"Hi Lisa, my name is Samantha. I am a professional freelance ghostwriter and copywriter. I enjoy competitive amateur athletics and spending time with my family. Thank you for this wonderful lesson on introductions."

"Hello, my dear young historians! I'm Ms. MacDonald, your new history teacher! This is my third year teaching high school world history online—it's a fascinating subject! I've read all of the *Twilight Saga* and finally started reading *Harry Potter* this week. I live in downtown Seattle, where I love to go to museums and concerts. Last month I went to the 30 Seconds to Mars concert. Where do you live? What are you into?"

(This introduction is for a discussion forum. Sherri Morgan MacDonald's online students live all over the state of Washington.)

"Hello Lisa, my name is Ian Williams and I, unfortunately, am not quite as fond of photography as you are. I do, however, enjoy riding my motorcycle around, absorbing the serenity a photo may convey. When I'm not riding, I work as a learning facilitator for a large pharmaceutical corporation."

"My name is Tina, Tina Clark. I am a nontraditional college of business student majoring in accounting. I am a mother of four grown boys, and my favorite activity is hiking with my new husband, although I don't get to do it as often as I would like."

"My name is Soumia. I am fifteen years old. I am Algerian and I study in secondary school."

"Me Tarzan. You Jane."

(This last one came from Lee Tsao, who used to be my manager.)

2. Conversation Magic:
How to Improve Your Conversation Skills

You start a conversation you can't even finish it. / You're talkin' a lot, but you're not sayin' anything.

—Talking Heads, "Psycho Killer"

When I was young, I remember being embarrassed by my mother—particularly when we were out in public. No, she never dressed funny (in fact she always looked impeccable), or chewed tobacco, or did anything out of the ordinary. What she did was indulge in her habit of starting conversations with strangers! (Horrors, right?)

She started conversations in supermarket lines, in the post office, in department stores, really anywhere. I remember one instance in which my siblings and I went to the park with my mom and our next-door neighbor's kids. That meant a total of nine kids and just my mom. During our outing, a woman said to my mom, "Hope you're having a good day at the park. Nice-looking kids. Are they all yours or is this a picnic?" My mother sarcastically replied, "Yes, they're all mine and it's *no* picnic!" I still remember the horrified look on the other woman's face and the big smile on my mom's face as she looked at us as if to say, "Shhh . . . let's enjoy this moment."

My mom let the woman suffer for a beat, then finally laughed and explained. It was a great way to break the ice and they ultimately became friends.

From this and countless other encounters with strangers, my mom showed me how to start conversations. The most important thing that she taught me was that strangers are no longer strangers once you talk to them. (Hmm, I wonder if that's why I do a weekly podcast that's like a conversation with thousands of strangers at once?)

Unfortunately, for many people conversation making doesn't come easily or naturally—it can be awkward or intimidating. Certainly for the text-messaging generation, in-person conversation-making seems to be a lost art.

Simply put, social conversation is how things get done. It's how we get to know people and get comfortable with them. It's how we build trust and credibility. Your ability to communicate naturally and spontaneously with *everyone* you meet is critical. It's a skill that will help you in just about every personal and professional situation and is perhaps the biggest determining factor in your success (or failure).

Take a minute to think about the most successful people you know. I bet the one thing they all have in common is the gift of gab. Successful people have an ability to engage anyone in conversation and consistently make him or her feel comfortable and connected within a very short period of time.

Here's the good news: This is a skill that can be developed, even for those who are extremely shy. For those who already think they are good at making conversation, this is a skill that can always be improved upon.

Quick Quiz: How do you feel about making conversation with strangers? Do you have any standard questions at the ready to help you start a conversation?

Let's start with the basics. Here are the six steps to conversation making.

Step 1: Cultivate a welcoming attitude.
Step 2: Pay attention to everyone and everything around you.
Step 3: Be genuinely curious and interested in other people.
Step 4: Listen and look for common ground.
Step 5: Ask open-ended follow-up questions.
Step 6: Share stories and appreciate your conversation partner.

Step #1: Cultivate a Welcoming Attitude

What do I mean by welcoming attitude? You need to let go of self-conscious and judgmental thinking. Don't worry about what you are going to say, how you look, or how the other person may perceive you. Instead, focus on them. Pay attention, listen carefully, and encourage them to share something of interest to them. Demonstrate your genuine interest in your conversation partner by giving him or her your full attention. Keep in mind, most people are happy to engage in a conversation and are relieved when someone else takes the lead.

You might even consider following Sam Walton's 10-foot Rule for Walmart employees: When you come within 10 feet of a person, look the person in the eye and greet them. According to Walmart's Web site[1], this was something he learned in college and practiced his entire life:

> I would always look ahead and speak to the person coming toward me. If I knew them, I would call them by name, but even if I didn't, I would still speak to them. Before long, I probably knew more students than anybody in the university and they recognized me, and considered me their friend.

This rule helped Walton to be successful in school and successful in business.

Welcoming also means that you don't dismiss people. Don't let things like clothes or office space (or book titles) fool you. Remember, Steve Jobs was once the awkward guy at parties always wearing a bad turtleneck and saying things like "Well, I've got some stuff rigged up in my garage . . ." Everyone has a story. Be the first to discover the great ones.

I already mentioned in the last chapter that I made the mistake of judging some people at an author conference based on the topics of their books. What I didn't say was that I also avoided talking with some of the other attendees because I felt a bit intimidated. In both cases, I missed opportunities. Ultimately I regretted my unconscious decision to not interact with certain people. From time to time, this happens to all of us.

Welcoming means you are available for and even encourage conversations with everyone. At times, we are tired and feel like we just don't have the mental energy to meet someone new. This is when I find myself suddenly needing to check and send e-mails or make phone calls. It's my way of letting myself off the hook—but the reality is that I have missed opportunities because I didn't make the effort.

Don't let that happen to you. Instead, remind yourself to be welcoming, even when you don't want to be because effective, genuine conversation-making is critical to your personal and professional success.

 Quick Quiz: Do you regularly greet those around you? Have you ever avoided meeting people at an event? Why? Is this a pattern for you?

Step #2: Pay Attention to Everyone and Everything Around You
Once you have cultivated your welcoming attitude, the next step is to pay attention to everyone and everything around you. If you are going to an event, Google its attendees ahead of time. Does

somebody have an interesting story? Is there someone who can introduce you to the person you *really* want to meet?

It's also always good to keep an eye on the headlines. Follow local and global news. You don't have to be an expert, just be aware. What's going on in the local news? In your industry?

What's going on in pop culture? (You'd be surprised how lively discussions can get about the latest episode of a reality TV show!) Remember that behind every name tag is a possible Adele worshipper, a would-be chef, or a football fan with a Tim Tebow bobblehead on their desk.

At an event, pay attention to what's around you—the traffic, the parking, the venue, the artwork, the theme, the food . . . everything. Do you see something unusual? Statement pieces make statements. And you'll always find them accompanied by someone who's excited to talk about them. Anything could become a statement piece. See that woman in the bright red jacket? It's unlikely that she casually threw that on, so compliment her on it. Is the VP of your department using GoodReader on the latest iPad? There's a good chance that VP loves it, so ask about it.

Step #3: Be Genuinely Curious and Interested in Other People

So once you've gathered your "intelligence," it's easy to do the next step. Be curious! It also helps to be energetic, have a willingness to take chances, and genuinely love to meet new people (but these aren't required).

Dale Carnegie, writer of the gold standard on literally *How to Win Friends and Influence People* said it this way: "You can make more friends in two months by becoming interested in other people than you can in two years by trying to get other people interested in you."

Most people want to have a pleasant conversation and consider that a difficult task. So take the lead by making a comment or asking a question (without interrogating). The key is to be genuinely interested and inquisitive. Use the research you gathered to ask relevant, interesting questions.

At an event, look for someone who is standing alone and who returns your eye contact. Or look for noisy groups, in which people appear to be enjoying themselves. It's likely your friendly advances will be welcomed.

A way to get good at this is to practice making conversations with strangers anytime you are able: in a supermarket line, while waiting for the bus or train, on a plane, in the doctor's office. Really, the more you practice, the easier it gets. But be sure your advances are welcome by paying careful attention to the reactions you receive.

I tend to use the same starter questions mostly because I like them and can remember them. In a professional setting I tend to use the following three the most:

- How did you get started in this [insert line of work/industry]?
- What do you most enjoy about your work?
- What advice would you give to someone working on/in [insert project/profession]?

Once I have established some rapport over professional matters, I generally prefer to move on to social questions. Here are my three favorite "any situation" conversation starters:

- What do you do when you're not doing this?
- What are you passionate about?
- What are your plans for the weekend? / What did you do over the weekend?

VIP Bonus: Download a list of twenty-five business and social *Smart Talk* conversation starters and get other exclusive information and benefits by joining my free members-only VIP site www.smarttalksuccess.com/VIP.

You don't need to memorize a long list, you just need to have one or two favorites. However, one option would be to keep a longer list on your mobile device for a quick refresher just before a networking event.

Of course, sometimes the other person will begin the conversation by asking you a question. In that case it's really easy to extend the conversation by first responding and then turning the question back on the other person by asking, "So, what do *you* think?" or "How about you?"

Another option for conversation making is to not rely on a chance meeting, but to instead plan on who would be a great addition to your network and invite them to have a conversation. Send an e-mail, and in the subject line you might put something along the lines of "introducing myself" or "invitation to have coffee." However a customized subject line is likely to get more attention. "From one hockey fan to another" (if you're both hockey fans) or "Idea To Help You." Better yet, have someone in your network introduce you.

Explain to the recipient why they're receiving an e-mail from you. In the body of the e-mail, very briefly describe your relevant background, state what you can offer them, and specify why you are interested in meeting them. If you are asking something of them, be sure you are asking quick questions or for short advice. You don't want them to feel like you want a full hour of their time or you are trying to get their professional services for free. Ask to meet at a specific time ("we should get together for coffee sometime" is too vague). Then, end with a sincere thank-you for considering your request.

For example, the e-mail may read something like this:

Hello Mr. Brown:

This is Joe Smith with the Metropolitan Historical Library. I recently read your article, "Unique Ways to Increase Funding for Historical Libraries" and see by your Web site that you will be in our city for a few weeks. I am very interested in meeting you to share some of what we are doing here at Metropolitan. I'd love to tell you how we are applying your ideas and would like to get your advice on how we might do it differently. Would you be free for coffee on Friday morning, September 15, at 9:00 a.m.? We have a café in the library and I would love to treat you.

Thank you for considering this. I look forward to hearing from you,

Joe Smith
Head Librarian
Metropolitan Historical Library

Most important, have the right motive for wanting to meet the other person—namely, to *mutually benefit* from the connection and shared knowledge. Don't put forth any further expectations.

When you meet in-person, once you've established initial contact or asked your favorite opening conversation starter, don't worry about what you are going to say next. Let the conversation unfold naturally.

Step #4: Listen and Look for Common Ground

It's so important that I'm going to say that twice; please, don't worry about what you are going to say next! After you ask a question or begin the conversation, just *listen*. Listen closely. It's one of the most important skills for effective conversation-making.

If you're thinking about what you are going to say next, you won't be listening carefully enough to the other person and you won't pick up on what's important to them or on any subtle signals your conversation partner may be sending. Listening carefully shows you are interested and is the best way to carry a conversation forward.

So what are you listening and looking for? You need to be listening to *what* your conversation partner is saying and also *how* they are saying it. You are listening for shared culture, environment, activities/interests, roles, goals, attitudes, values, and beliefs. You're listening for excitement in their voice. You're looking at posture. You're looking for a sparkle in their eyes or a smile on their face. You're looking at the eyes, the mouth, and the eyebrows for clues as to how someone is feeling. For example, a constant stare with immobile facial muscles indicates coldness, while a natural Duchenne smile (look for wrinkles around the eyes and uplifted cheeks) indicates pleasure. In fact, despite cultural differences, when it comes to smiling, most people perceive a natural smile as expressing positive interest.

Check This Out: Test your ability to spot the difference between a fake smile and a real one. Visit www.smarttalk success.com/extras.

Your goal is to use these cues to figure out what is important and exciting for the other person. What do their words say about their attitudes, beliefs, and values? The initial question simply touches the outer surface; the subsequent questions dig in deeper.

Step #5: Ask Open-Ended, Follow-Up Questions
One big reason why conversations run out of steam is because neither person is talking about anything that is really important to them. You can avoid that awkward and embarrassing feeling by drawing out the other person. Advance the conversation by asking open-ended, follow-up questions. It's best to ask a question that is an extension of something your partner just said. If you can't formulate a question, here are some standard follow-ups you can always use:

"Wow! Really? Can you give me an example?"
"Hmm, I'm not sure I fully understand. What do you mean when you say . . . ?"
"Can you elaborate on that?"
"What happened after that?"
"Tell me more."
"How did you get interested in that?"

These types of questions allow your conversation partner to easily move the conversation forward. To move the conversation even deeper, you can ask a different sort of follow-up question:

"How did you feel when . . . [insert topic they were just talking about]"

"Why do you think that's important to you?"

"Interesting, do you think you would have answered the same way five years ago?"

"Why is that?"

Step #6: Share Your Stories and Appreciate

 Warning: Don't solely ask questions and listen—that will feel like an interrogation to your conversation partner. This must be a two-way street to be effective.

Also, avoid questions that only require a one-word response. If you're asked a question that only requires a one-word response, respond but fill in more details by sharing a story of your own. Share an example or further explanation. You need to tell your own stories so your conversation partner also understands and feels how your "circles" overlap. It's through our stories that we share our values, beliefs, attitudes, roles, goals, activities/interests, environment, and culture. It's through our stories that we connect.

Research suggests[2] that self-disclosure is a fundamental way that relationship bonds are established, developed, and maintained. Researchers[3,4] have examined the "disclosure reciprocity" effect, or the tendency for interaction partners to disclose information in a reciprocal fashion.

In fact, partners feel a pressure or obligation to reciprocate the intimacy level of information that is shared. It's the way we deepen our relationships. One person's disclosure encourages another's disclosure, which in turn, may encourage the first person to disclose more, and so on. This is how we learn about others and develop relationships.

When starting a conversation with a new person, it's important to keep your stories interesting and light. The idea is to slowly move deeper through the conversational levels. The operative word here is "slowly." Your last doctor's visit, the argument you had with your spouse, and that weird rash have one thing in common: they're too much information. Telling someone something too soon can make them feel uncomfortable and inhibit the development of the relationship.

 Warning: The beginning of conversation is not the time to verbally offer your autobiography or to discuss deeply held beliefs, values, or very personal/private matters.

A goal of conversation making is to encourage gradual self-disclosure. During your conversation you'll want to nod, make eye contact, and smile appropriately. Engage your partner by saying, "Tell me more . . ." or repeat some items back with phrases such as, "So, if I understand correctly, you recommend . . ."

Research[5] shows that as relationships develop over time self-disclosure progresses in depth (sensitivity of material disclosed) and breadth (variety of topics discussed). For some people you meet you it will be very comfortable to rapidly broaden and deepen your conversation, while others will prefer you move slowly.

Your decision to disclose information is based on a number of fundamental factors[6] such as your culture, your social network, and your personality. However, it also depends on your assessment of the specific conversation. For example, does the disclosure fit in with the flow of the conversation? How do you anticipate the other person will respond? Does it fit within the privacy levels of the conversation or the quality of the relationship? Of course, it's also based on how your conversation partner reacted to other information you have disclosed.

This link between self-disclosure and closeness is the *art* of conversation-making. People disclose more to someone who they like, to someone who discloses to them, and to someone to whom they've disclosed personal information[7]. So, this is the iterative process for building stronger relationships and trust. Perhaps most important for business professionals, people buy from people they know, like, and trust.

Finally, it's important to recognize that not all in-person conversations are comfortable. You most likely will not be standing in front of your future best friend. Your goal is to remain friendly and curious and if a genuine connection isn't formed, that's OK.

However, not all conversations are started and developed in person. Particularly today, with the staggering growth of social media, conversations are often started online. (I went to a conference recently and was pleasantly surprised to meet *in-person* seven people that I already "knew" from our online conversations.)

I know the art of online conversation-making is gaining mainstream status because my clients have been asking about how to make and extend online conversations more and more. They want to understand how to engage their audience and build their brand via the Web. The core principles are the same. In fact, trust is the currency of the Internet. However, there is an art, a separate art, of Web interaction and conversation-making.

How to Start a Conversation Via the Web

First, a disclaimer: What I'm about to share with you, I learned through experience. So, you'll need to do a little trial and error to analyze for yourself what works and what doesn't in your specific situation.

Keep the Introduction Simple
When you meet someone online, often you don't need (or want) to include too much information—usually just your name, the reason you are contacting, and a link to your About page or online

profile. This way if the person wants to know more, they can just click.

However, beyond the initial introduction, you'll want to enter into conversations.

Keep It Two-Sided

It may seem simple and obvious, but a fundamental concept that many people tend to forget is that Web conversations are two-sided. Social media conversations are *interactions* between people; it's not about collecting friends. Yes, it is important to broadcast links (push marketing) that drive traffic to your Web site; however, it's equally important, if not more so, to listen, to ask questions, to solicit opinions, and to get others to rebroadcast your key messages. You need to respond, to interact, to be visible. The easiest and simplest way to do that is to comment on other people's social media updates or participate in online forums by answering questions.

Solicit Opinions

The NBA Facebook fan page is a great example of an organization that gets online conversation right. Even if you are not a basketball fan, I suggest you "like" their page because you'll learn a ton of effective techniques for making online conversation and engaging an audience. Here's a great example: They posted, "As good as it gets! Tonight is for all the marbles. Who will win Game 7?" and added a Facebook application to poll for results.

It was interesting to me that although hundreds of people participated in the poll, many more people responded in the comments. The site achieved significant engagement with that simple question. So what's the lesson? On the Web, people will often respond to questions that have no right or wrong answer—especially if it's something they are passionate about. By asking for personal opinion, the site manages to tap into people's willingness to respond both to the original question and to the opinions of other fans.

Post Videos or Photos

Another way to generate more conversations is to post videos and photos, particularly on Facebook, Google+, YouTube, and Pinterest. Again, if you look to the NBA Facebook page, you'll see a prime example of that. They've incorporated a montage of photos, which when clicked lead to related video clips.

It seems our attention spans are getting shorter and shorter. Take advantage of this. A vast majority of internet users prefer watching a video to reading an article. Short (less than three minutes) videos that are entertaining, directly related to your topic area, and that include very subtle shameless marketing are perfect.

Reward Commitment to Your Brand

Another obvious way to generate interaction is rewarding commitment to your brand by providing free samples or products and services exclusively available via these social media interactions. After all, that's why most people initially join the conversation to begin with—because they are interested in additional related content, possible freebies, and additional opportunities to engage with your brand they wouldn't have through traditional channels.

For example, the NBA's Philadelphia 76ers basketball team ran a contest to choose their next mascot: Big Ben, B. Franklin Dogg, or Phil E. Moose. Fans Jerry Rizzo and Hunter Coleman joined the conversation by creating Twitter accounts on behalf of the possible new mascots.

The Twitter introduction for Phil E. Moose read, "Just your average slam-dunking moose trying to make it in the City of Brotherly Love as the future mascot of the @Sixers." The tweets Rizzo and Coleman created were equally clever.

When these profiles began to gain attention, the team sent an e-mail to Rizzo asking him to stop tweeting. However, the 76ers CEO Adam Aron recognized the situation as an opportunity to reward Rizzo's commitment to the brand, and to show support for this enthusiastic, clever fan. Aron reviewed Jerry's online portfolio, interviewed him, and ultimately offered him a position as the team's social media coordinator.

Now that's an awesome reward for an equally incredible show of brand commitment. It also highlights another important part of conversation-making. You can't always control an online conversation and you need to be ready to go wherever the conversation leads you.

Hold Contests

This story also demonstrates that holding a contest is a great way to generate conversation and enthusiasm. In June of 2010, Oprah Winfrey's cable network, OWN, ran a "Your OWN Show" video contest. The winners then participated in a reality TV series to see who would ultimately get their own show on OWN. I'm guessing that you probably heard about the contest at the time—either because someone asked you to vote, you saw an entry on someone's Facebook page, or you heard about it through the news or a podcast.

The point is, online contests tend to generate a lot of conversation among the participants *and* their friends and family. To encourage voting, participants talk socially about the contest through blog posts, status updates, and comments that then create more conversations, indirectly exposing more people to the brand. Most important, these online conversations generate word-of-mouth buzz!

Deliver Free Presentations

You can also create interest in your products and services through public presentations of your work (both online and in-person). Webinars and conference calls can help expand your reach and allow you to build a stronger relationship with your current customers and with potential customers. By sharing your passion for your work, your attendees will experience your enthusiasm and expertise first hand. This in itself can set you apart from the competition and create word-of-mouth buzz. When you present yourself publically and make a great first impression, you're developing trust. And most businesses need to earn the trust of their prospects before they are hired for the job.

In my business, I often work with partners to deliver free webinars because they're inexpensive and easy to organize. By partnering with organizations that have large customer bases, I am able to get exposure to a large number of potential prospects while at the same time my partner extends his ongoing conversation with his customers by providing value-added content. We work together to extend our conversations and build trust and good will.

Another option would be to look to organizations and individuals that already host a regular webinar or podcast series. Look for series that you enjoy and that attract the right demographics for your industry niche. Then pitch them on why your content would be beneficial to their audience.

Keep in mind, however, that the actual presentation is only one step in the process. The idea is to collect contact information so that you can engage with your audience before and after your program to provide a more personalized experience.

Throw a Twitter Party or an E-meet and Greet

Don't worry I hear you: "Wait, a what? What's a Twitter party?"

Twitter parties are just another online event you can use to meet new prospects, launch a product, announce a service, meet customers, or just get people talking. They are very cheap and easy to put together and can generate a lot of online buzz. Attendees love them because they're fun, low pressure, and no one has to get dressed up or even brush their hair. The key is to keep them fun, informative, highly interactive, and to have a little something to offer.

What I'm talking about is a prearranged online chat that happens through the use of Twitter updates (or tweets) that include a predefined keyword (called a hashtag) to link the tweets together in a virtual conversation. It's sometimes called a tweet chat and usually includes a leader and a guest "speaker."

For example, my friend Melinda Emerson, also known as Small Biz Lady, interviews small business experts every Wednesday night, at 8 P.M. EST using Twitter @SmallBizChat. Through tweets, Melinda asks her guest experts a series of questions, which are then answered in tweets. Using Twitter as a tool allows anyone to follow the conversation and to ask questions.

I'll admit it, this format can take a bit of getting used to. The information flows quickly and in 140 characters or less, but it is a great way to engage many people in a conversation. Melinda adds a nice touch to her chats. She invites attendees to introduce themselves at the end of the program and encourages them to follow people they found interesting to continue the conversation.

 Check This Out: Visit www.smarttalksuccess.com /extras to get a free guide to online conversation-making, and a discount to Lisa's "Making Money Through Online Conversations" webinar.

Summary: How to Improve Your Conversation Skills

✓ Conversations and disclosures are what lead to relationships and are how things get done.

✓ Steps to In-Person Conversation-Making
  ▸ Cultivate a welcoming attitude.
  ▸ Pay attention to everyone and everything around you.
  ▸ Be genuinely curious and interested in other people.
  ▸ Listen and look for common ground.
  ▸ Ask open-ended, follow-up questions.
  ▸ Share stories and appreciate.

✓ Techniques For Online Conversations
  ▸ Keep introductions simple.
  ▸ Keep conversations two-sided.

- ▶ Solicit opinions.
- ▶ Post videos or photos.
- ▶ Reward commitment to your brand.
- ▶ Hold contests.
- ▶ Deliver free presentations.
- ▶ Throw a Twitter party.

I have provided you with actionable recommendations to help create meaningful conversations. Your ability to make masterful conversations will develop through persistent practice. It's up to you to execute. It's up to you to connect.

Smart Talk Challenge #1

Create two questions you can use in any situation to start a conversation. Create two questions you can use in a professional setting to start a conversation. Try them out. Modify as needed.

Smart Talk Challenge #2

Choose a venue (coffee shop, classroom, meet-up) and see how many strangers you can connect with in one day. By flexing your conversation muscle every day, this will get easier to do.

Smart Talk Challenge #3

Choose one or two of the methods of online conversation-making described above and give it a try. Experiment with different techniques when using different tools to see what works best where.

Case Study: Angela Lauria

Angela Lauria created a teleseminar script to introduce herself, her business partner, and a new product. Angela assumed the role of moderator and host but did not share much about who she was, instead focusing on her partner and the product.

She asked me to help her revise the script because she received feedback that audience members were left wondering who exactly Angela was and why she was part of the teleseminar. Bottom line, they didn't trust her.

It was clear to me that Angela needed to increase her self-disclosure. I suggested that Angela describe her genuine emotional commitment to the shared values and goals of her audience. Specifically, I suggested she tell a story that showed that her values and beliefs about her topic were the same as the attendees'. I suggested she tell a story that would make it crystal clear to anyone listening that she was "one of them." In essence, I was asking her to share areas where I felt her circles would overlap with those in the audience. You can read how she changed her script to better connect with her audience. What a difference!

VIP Bonus: Download the original script, the revised script, and other exclusive information and benefits by joining my *free* members-only VIP site: www.smarttalksuccess .com/VIP.

3. Cat Got Your Tongue?
What to Say When . . .

It usually takes me more than three weeks to prepare a good impromptu speech.

—Mark Twain

Vincenza's husband passed away. Many people brought her food, sent her flowers, and helped her make arrangements. She wanted to thank everyone for their support, but she just didn't know what to say.

Lorraine's friend was going through a divorce. Every time she thought of her friend she felt bad, but just didn't know what to say.

Mallory was asked to make a toast at her sister's wedding. She loves her sister very much, but doesn't know her soon-to-be husband. She's nervous about the speech because she's not sure what to say.

 Quick Quiz: Have you ever been in a situation where you just didn't know what to say? What did you do to gather your thoughts? When you finally said something, did you adequately express your feelings?

I've noticed from the hundreds of e-mails that I've received from listeners and readers of my work that there are some universal situations that many of us seem to struggle with from time to time. So I decided to devote an entire chapter to the top five most common, "What do I say when . . ." questions that I have received over the years.

- What do I say when . . . someone is going through a tough time?
- What do I say when . . . I make a toast?
- What do I say when . . . I attend a work party?
- What do I say when . . . I introduce someone?
- What do I say when . . . I write a thank-you note?

Before I cover the specifics of each situation, I want to mention that when you are in a situation where you are not quite sure what to say, the most important thing is to not get hung up on struggling to come up with the right words.

Instead, focus on the other person by listening carefully. That way, you will then be able to express yourself naturally and sincerely. Just by listening, acknowledging, and respecting, we can make others feel special. With this in mind, allow me to address each specific situation.

. . . Someone Is Going Through a Hard Time

I know from my personal experience that when someone is going through a really tough time (death in the family, illness, divorce, etc.) it can make the people around him or her feel uncomfortable. I lost my late husband in 1995, my mom in 2000, and my dad in 2011, so I saw firsthand how these situations can leave ordinarily talkative people tongue-tied or feeling helpless. Many have told me that they had no idea what to say, what to do, or how to help.

So in this situation, the most important communication tip is . . . respond. Any words or actions are better than nothing. Don't disappear. Some people are so uncomfortable with a tragic situation that they say nothing at all. They either ignore the issue or they retreat from the friendship all together.

With time, the situation gets worse. Because they retreated, they're embarrassed, and they disappear completely. Although it's understandable, it doesn't help. Always keep in mind, your goal is to deepen relationships by acknowledging when others are experiencing difficulties and to respect their feelings, no matter what they are.

Be There

It may surprise you to learn that one way to acknowledge another person's pain is just be there. You don't have to give advice or think of clever things to say to make them smile. You don't have to discuss feelings. You don't need to have the answers. Sometimes, all you need to do is be there—to listen.

Sometimes you will only hear silence. That's OK. Invite them to lunch, dinner, or your home. Sit quietly together. Call them every two weeks to leave a message that says you are thinking about them. Even if they never return your call, they will know you care. Let them grieve in their own way. Be there. Don't retreat. Don't disappear.

Respond to What You Hear

When it's time to speak, respond to the specific words and feelings expressed. Everyone experiences a death in the family, serious illness, or divorce very differently. And it's even likely that same person experiences the pain differently from day to day, or even from moment to moment. So listen and respond to what the other person is experiencing in that particular moment.

Of course, there's no one right way to talk to someone who is going through the grieving process. And to be clear, each of these involves grieving a loss. An illness, a loss of a person, or a loss of abilities are all significant losses. All can be equally devastating to the person experiencing them.

Acknowledge the Loss

Every person who experiences a loss needs to have that loss recognized. Something as simple as, "I'm sorry that you are experiencing X—that just sucks. How are you feeling?" If you are uncomfortable verbally expressing yourself, then send a handwritten note or book written to help others with the loss, or perhaps just a copy of your favorite quote. Sending a card, note, or book is always a good idea because it can provide comfort that you may not be able to, it can also provide comfort when you are not available, potentially for many years to come.

And don't just send one thing. Over time send a few different things to show the person that you recognize the significance of their loss, that you haven't forgotten, and that you care.

Offer Your Sincere Support

It's OK to offer generic support. "Let me know if there is anything I can do." Or "I'm sorry that you are going through this difficult time. Tell me how I can help."

But perhaps a better idea is to offer specific support. For a friend you might say, "If you'd like I can bring over a few precooked meals, or I could run a few errands for you." For a work colleague, you might say, "Can I bring you some lunch?" Don't push; just offer your support in the best way you can.

If you are at a loss for words, try "I don't know what to say," or "I can't imagine what you are going through," or "It must be horrible." By the way, it's not a good idea to say you know how it feels (even if you have had a similar experience). Every situation is different and every person experiences grief differently. Comparing your experience to theirs may just make the person feel more alone.

Share Your Happy Memories

After a month or two has passed since the main event, many people don't want "to bring it up." They fear they might make things worse. But the reality is, significant events like these are never far from the mind anyway. So don't be afraid to ask how things are going and to directly address the loss.

For example, after a death, don't be afraid to share your happy memories. I learned so many things I never knew about my relatives who passed away: things that made me proud, things that made me smile, and things that helped me feel closer to them even though they were gone. These emotional gifts are precious.

Warning: In the case of a divorce be careful not to share negative stories about the person they are divorcing. Now is not the time to let your friend know that you never really liked their spouse.

So when someone is going through a difficult loss, it's important to first listen. Listen carefully so that you can respond directly to the thoughts, feelings, and emotions being shared in the moment. Always acknowledge the loss and offer your sincere support and don't be afraid to share happy memories.

In fact, happy memories are not only good to share in times of grief, but also in times of celebration. Interestingly, celebrations are also a time when we often find ourselves at a loss for words.

. . . I Need to Make a Toast?

In particular, people sometimes struggle when called upon to make a toast.

The first step, before you even begin to write a toast, is to brainstorm a few ideas so that you have some material to choose from. Record a few positive qualities that you admire in the person or qualities you value in your relationship with him or her. Be sure to think about short stories that are examples of those positive traits. Finally, write down any shared memories that are heartfelt or funny.

Warning: Though the memories should be funny they shouldn't be mean. It's a toast, not a roast. This is not the time to bring up embarrassing or hurtful memories. That is a sure-fire way to sour a nice moment.

Once you have a few ideas to choose from, select your best material to develop the toast. Always start by introducing yourself and defining your relationship to the person, then transition to a story or memory. If you don't have one, you can move directly to two or three traits that you admire. Be sure to include a brief story that is an example of each trait. Finally wrap it up with a wish or blessing.

Should You Use Notes During a Toast?

Of course, practicing is always a good idea, but if you are afraid you might forget what to say, it's okay to bring some small note cards with you. Remember, even if you are still feeling a little jittery, it's very important to be sober when you deliver your toast.

Before you deliver your toast, be sure that everyone has a full glass. Don't tap your glass to get attention, simply raise it and state that it is time for a toast. Once you begin your toast, you can bring your glass back down again.

Delivering Your Toast

At this point, even if you're nervous, it's important to look and act confident. Maintain good posture and use a strong voice. When you start, look directly into the eyes of the person you are honoring. Of course, you'll need to give everyone some eye contact, especially when you are telling them who you are, but be sure to look back to the honoree when you tell your stories. Most of the toast should be delivered directly to the honoree, but some eye contact can be shared with everyone.

Be Polite, Personal, Simple, and Sincere

You'll want to keep the toast short, three or four minutes maximum, especially if others are toasting as well. If you speak for more than a few minutes, the focus of the toast shifts to you. The key is to remain polite, personal, simple, and sincere.

Just be who you are. Want to see a room full of people collectively squirm? Try and be someone you aren't. Are you funny? Then toasting funny will come naturally and will be much appreciated by the person being honored. Trying-to-be-funny lines delivered by a not-too-funny person . . . awkward! Do you have a gift for poetry? Great. Create an original poem and the honoree will be touched. If not, then don't deliver a cringe-worthy toast by pretending as if you have the flair of Thoreau.

If it feels like you are trying too hard, then you probably are. On the other hand, if you deliver a sincere toast from your heart, it will be a big success. Consider bringing tissues along. You might need them if you do a good job of telling a heartfelt story.

How to End a Toast

When you are finished with the toast, don't forget to raise your glass again and nod first toward the audience and then toward the honoree. It is not always appropriate to clink glasses. In a large group with vast amounts of space or tables between guests, it's completely appropriate to raise your glass and make eye contact with those around you.

Once the one being toasted has been acknowledged, take a sip of your drink.

 Warning: The honoree is not expected to drink. It would be the equivalent of applauding for yourself.

Again, this is the time to honor (not embarrass). Share funny and heartfelt stories to illustrate the qualities you value in the honoree and in your friendship. Most important be yourself. Speak naturally and confidently, after all, you were chosen to deliver the toast for a reason.

Another celebration that people often struggle with is the office or work party. (What's that? Did I just hear you say, "Ugh!")

. . . I Need to Attend a Work Party?

If you're like me, you've been tempted to blow off an office party.

Don't.

Missing work parties is like missing important work meetings. I know, I know, you don't get paid to attend, but it can cost you if you don't.

On the other hand, attending an office party can pay off if you use your time wisely. Office parties give you the chance to talk with people you normally don't interact with. You may make some important connections and you'll be seen as a team player. Besides, work parties are an opportunity to practice and master your mingling skills.

Perhaps most important, keep in mind at all times that it is an *office* party, not an office *party*. Yes, it is a social celebration to some degree, but I'd suggest wearing your thinking cap and not your party hat because it can affect your career prospects. A 2010 poll[1] by human resource firm Adecco reported that 14 percent of employees say they know someone who has been fired due to bad behavior at a holiday party and 40 percent of us have seen or suffered a major indiscretion at a work-sponsored holiday event. So your goal for any office party should be to expand your internal network and deepen your existing professional relationships, while limiting your alcohol consumption because too much alcohol often leads to poor decision-making.

 Check This Out: Read a few true holiday horror stories by visiting www.smarttalksuccess.com/extras.

Set Networking Goals

While it's fun to interact with your best work buds, office parties are a great opportunity to get to know people from other departments that you do not cross paths with you regularly. It never hurts to have rapport with the accounting department or the engineering team even if your work is creative!

However, before you set off, decide your goals for the event. For example, "I'd like to meet eight new people," or "I'd like to further develop my relationship with George and Sally from accounting," or "I'd like to connect with some of the folks in the graphics department."

Show Genuine Interest

You can start a conversation with someone you don't know well by asking him or her to tell you more about what they do (inside or outside of work). Always spend a portion of your time with a handful of people unfamiliar to you. You'll come away from the party with a gift—some new connections!

For those you already know, you can always start a conversation by asking, "How is your latest project going?" But you may prefer to take advantage of the social setting to talk about something other than work. Usually parties include food, so it's easy to ease into a conversation with a food-related question: "What do you think of these crab cakes?" or "Do you cook much?" or "What is your favorite type of food?"

Another approach is to consider giving a *sincere* compliment. Mention a specific contribution that you find valuable. For example, "Charlie, I always enjoy your sense of humor. It lightens the atmosphere when we are under a lot of stress. Thanks so much."

 Warning: It is important that the compliment is genuine, otherwise you will seem condescending—not the impression you want to make.

Just remember to stay positive. Don't share what you really think about the tasteless food or the tacky venue. It's also not the time for office gossip, or even gossip about people who left the company. Professional mingling is about sharing small stuff and letting the conversation grow naturally. Let your curiosity and genuine interest guide the conversation in a positive direction.

Be sure that you connect with your boss and the most senior person at the event, even if just to say good night and to thank them for the event.

Follow-Up

The party is just the start to cultivating new relationships. You'll need to follow-up to develop them. Many people get stuck at this point because they don't know how to deepen the initial contact. They often think the next interaction needs to be significant, but in reality, what is more important is continued consistent interaction. For example, send a simple note, something like, "I really enjoyed getting to know you better. I particularly enjoyed learning about XYZ."

Follow these tips to turn the dreaded office party into an effective work meeting. Start by setting networking goals for the event, while there show genuine interest, and follow-up afterwards.

And before the party, brush up on your introduction skills.

... I Need to Introduce Someone?

None of us like "social limbo." That's when you're with a colleague or friend and someone new walks up and engages your friend in a lively conversation. You have no idea who this person is or how they are connected, so you just stand by, in awkward silence. Of course, you could solve the problem by introducing yourself, but the situation could have been much smoother had your friend properly introduced you first.

The Main Rule of Introductions

The main goal of most professional introductions is to make everyone feel comfortable and to show respect. This means in a social setting you introduce a man to a woman, younger people to older people, and household members to guests. In a professional setting, you introduce a person of lower rank to a person of higher rank or of equal rank, the person you don't know as well to the person you know better.

The Process of Introduction

1. First, state the name of the *person being introduced to* (the higher-rank person) and say, "George, I would like to introduce . . ." or, "please meet . . ." or, "this is . . ." (If you don't know/remember the name of the higher-rank person, you can say, "Have you met my friend . . .")
2. Then, state the name of the *person being introduced.* This is the lower-ranking person. "Mr. Smith, have you met Mr. Jeff Walker?" (By the way, a simple rule of thumb is to refer to someone's name as you typically do.)
3. In a professional setting, you'll typically also want to include a brief mention of the titles or roles. "Mr. Smith, have you met my client Mr. Jeff Walker, the CEO of Advanta?"
4. Finally, it's great if you can include a brief mention of a topic of common interest between the two parties. However, don't elaborate. Your goal is to enable instant rapport and allow the pair to drive the ensuing conversation.

A Few Examples

- How to introduce a younger person to an older person: "Grandma Vincenza, please meet Linda and Larissa, they are both in Daniela's class."
- How to introduce a junior professional to a senior professional: "Mr. Kaplin, I would like to introduce Lou Crocetto, our newest intern."

- How to introduce an employee to a customer: "Ms. Marshall, I would like to introduce our operations team. This is Sue Charles, Jessie Rios, and Zoe Ogilvie. All three participated in last week's teleconference regarding our upcoming seminar."
- How to introduce a host to a guest: "Lee, I don't think you've met my sister, Debbie. Debbie lives in Washington, DC, but visits here frequently. Lee is my new VP of Operations."
- How to introduce a peer from your company to a peer from another organization: "Armando, I would like you to meet Hilmer Rivera, our VP of Sales. Hilmer, Armando Velasquez is a Director of Operations at TA Instruments."

Introducing an Expert

When introducing an expert to someone who will be paying for the expert's advice, the main goal of the introduction is different. Yes, it's still a gesture of respect, but primarily it's to make the person meeting the expert feel comfortable by building up the expert's credibility and likability.

Dr. Ken Flowe, an emergency room physician, provided the following example of what he would say to a patient he was admitting into the hospital:

"I just talked with Dr. Park, and he agreed that you needed to be admitted. He was happy to take care of you. We've worked together on lots of patients with the same condition that you have. He's really smart, very caring, and does a great job. You'll like him."

The final area of communication that I often get asked about is thank-you notes.

. . . I Need to Write a Thank-You Note?

Of course, the primary reason for sending a thank-you note is to show your gratitude. Appreciation and thankfulness are important in all relationships. A sincerely written thank-you note can deepen both professional and personal relationships. Besides, it's just plain mannerly to articulate your appreciation by thanking someone who has given you a gift, of help or time.

The Main Rules of Thank-You Notes

When should you send a thank-you? I'll leave the formal etiquette rules to the Quick and Dirty Tips' Modern Manners Guy. However, from a professional communication perspective, always send a handwritten thank-you note when someone gives you their time or hospitality.

 Warning: If possible, send a handwritten note, not an e-mail. Even if you have poor handwriting (like mine), still try to put pen to paper. The time it takes to write the note is part of your appreciation.

Finally, send the note promptly. Ideally, it should arrive within one week of the event/gift and certainly no more than two months after. I think some people postpone because they have so many to write, they just get overwhelmed and don't know where to begin. Others postpone because they aren't sure what to say.

I suggest writing only a few notes at a time, so that you're tackling a manageable task, rather than all at once which can seem daunting. Set up a convenient area in plain sight stocked with blue-black pens, blank cards, postcards, and stamps. This way you'll be reminded to complete your thank-you's and won't have any excuses. Keep a copy of the following five steps for writing a thank-you note on hand. This way, you'll always be motivated, prepared and never miss an opportunity to share your appreciation.

Five Simple Steps to Writing a Thank-You Note

Step #1: Greet the Gift Giver

The first step is the easiest. Choose a greeting and use the person's name: "Hello, Marty," "Hi, Susan," "Hello, Mr. Velasquez," "Hey, Sis."

Step #2: Generally Thank the Person for Their Kindness

The second step should be obvious: thank them for the gift. Maybe they gave you helpful advice, maybe they gave you a monetary gift, or maybe they spent time with you (like an interview). The idea is to explicitly recognize what you appreciated. This part of the thank-you is very general. For example:

> Hello, Marty,
> Thank you for the opportunity to meet with you this past Tuesday.

> Hi, Susan,
> I can't tell you how much I appreciated the chocolate-covered strawberries that you sent over.

> Hello, Mr. Velasquez,
> Thank you for the pay raise.

Step #3: Specifically Explain Why You Are Thankful

Step three is usually the most personal part of the note, and it should be unique for each note that you write. In this next sentence or two, you should get very specific. Tell the person why you are thankful. Share a detail you learned during the conversation, or perhaps a few specific reasons why you're thankful. This is the main part of your note and cannot be skipped.

 Warning: If you write thank-you's in advance, you are skipping this very important step. This does not show appreciation for the gift and your note won't have as strong an impact.

[Examples continued . . .]

[Marty note]
The fact that you and Joe share an office indicates the close working relationship that you two have built. I was also very

impressed by your strong business acumen, your communication skills, and your professionalism.

[Susan note]
> That was just what I needed to lift my spirits. The girls especially enjoyed sharing them with me.

[Mr. Velasquez note]
> This genuinely makes me feel my work is appreciated and that is very important to me.

Step #4: Share How You Will Use the Gift

Step four is to say how you will use or how you used the gift. If the gift was cash, don't elaborate on the specifics of what you will buy. Just simply say, "Your generous gift will certainly help when we go to buy our new car/home/blender." For gifts of time, simply state what you most valued about the time you spent together.

[Examples continued . . .]

[Marty note]
> As we discussed, I strongly support following a strategic sales process. I am confident that I can leverage my previous strategic experience to creatively, effectively, and consistently work with your team to drive results.

[Susan note]
> We ate them so fast, that Tim didn't even get a chance to have any! They were gone before he got home from work.

[Mr. Velasquez note]
> The extra money will really help us with household essentials, especially as our family is growing.

Step #5: Mention Future Interactions While Thanking Once More
The idea of this part of the note is to mention that you would like
to continue the relationship with the other party in some way.
Don't worry if you see them infrequently.

[Examples continued . . .]

[Marty note]

I hope you'll strongly consider my application. I would love to
work with you. Thanks again for the interview.

[Susan note]

I'll call you soon. Just wanted to thank you again for the yummy
treat.

[Mr. Velasquez note continued . . .]

I really enjoy working with you and I am looking forward to
more exciting challenges. Thanks again for the raise.

When you follow these five steps, writing an effective thank-
you note is easy. First greet the person and express your general
gratitude. Then specifically explain why you are thankful and how
you will use the gift. Finally, wrap up by mentioning future interactions and add one final thank-you.

Summary: What to Say When . . .

✓ When someone is going through a hard time:
  ▸ Don't ignore the situation, respond in some way.
  ▸ Be there.
  ▸ Listen.
  ▸ Acknowledge the loss.
  ▸ Offer your sincere support.
  ▸ Share happy memories.
✓ When you need to make a toast:
  ▸ It's OK to use notes.

- ▸ Use good posture and a strong voice.
- ▸ Be polite, personal, simple, and sincere.
- ▸ End by raising your glass.

✓ When you need to attend a work party:
- ▸ Attend.
- ▸ Wear your thinking cap, not your party hat.
- ▸ Set networking goals.
- ▸ Show genuine interest in your colleagues.
- ▸ Follow-up after the party.

✓ When you need to introduce someone:
- ▸ Make everyone comfortable and show respect.
- ▸ Follow introduction guidelines starting with higher ranking person.

✓ When you need to send a thank-you note:
- ▸ Send handwritten notes promptly.
- ▸ Greet the gift giver.
- ▸ Thank the person for their kindness.
- ▸ State why you are thankful.
- ▸ Share how you'll use the gift.
- ▸ Mention possible future interactions while thanking once more.

4. Giddyup Your Follow-Up: How to Effectively Follow Up on Your Conversations

You cannot guarantee good fruits from a tree which has not been properly taken care of.

—Martin Johnson

George has some clients he worked with about a year ago. He wanted to stay in touch with them, but procrastinated because he never felt like he had anything significant to say. He also felt socially awkward reaching out via e-mail and in person, so he ended up never following up. He wonders: Is it too late to contact them now?

Gary is looking for a new job. He starts networking by posting his résumé online, updating his social media profiles and adding new connections. He also decides to start a blog. He knows that most jobs come through networking and doesn't understand why his networking efforts aren't resulting in any progress.

Sue attends a conference. She meets some great people. She sincerely wants to follow-up with them, so she exchanges business cards and promises to keep in touch. Two weeks later, Sue sees the stack of cards she collected on her desk and wonders when she'll have the time to follow up. Three months later the cards are still there. She flips one over and tries to read her notes on the back, but she can't decipher her own handwriting. Sue wonders what she can do now.

 Quick Quiz: How often do you use the business cards you've collected? What holds you back from consistent follow-up?

Perhaps you've heard the adage, "The fortune is in the follow-up." Particularly today, we are all way too busy and way too distracted to remember much of anything after seeing it only once or twice. Without follow-up no matter how awesome you think you are or how much you might be able to serve a person, he or she simply won't remember you and the relationship will stagnate or end.

Interactions—small, consistent, and persistent interactions—are what build and strengthen relationships. Networking (or follow-up) is about your ability to remain relevant and to continue to provide value. It's about being genuinely curious and genuinely giving. Relationships will continue only as long as both parties derive value from the interaction. Follow-up activity is a marathon, not a sprint.

Lots of us get stuck investing time and effort, adding more and more contacts or following up just once after initial contact. However, it's equally important, if not *more important*, to patiently, persistently, and professionally continue your conversations. Follow-up conversations are what transform initial chitchat into solid connections and ultimately what transforms solid connections into professional relationships. It takes time for alliances to mature.

In fact, marketers know that small interactions define how a consumer will feel about a brand on the "gut" or emotional level. According to advertising research, most people need to hear a message at least nine times before deciding to take the next step— but it might take, eleven, fifteen, or even twenty-seven times![1] We need repetition to reinforce ideas. We need repetition to be memorable.

This concept can be applied to any kind of sales; whether you're selling products and services, looking for a job, or asking for a date. Consistent and patient professional follow-up is what seals the deal. Those who do consistently and patiently follow up reap significant rewards; unfortunately, most of us do not.

So, if follow-up is so powerful, then why do so many of us fail to do it? Perhaps it is a fear of being rejected; maybe we feel like follow-up is being bothersome; or maybe we think if someone is interested, they will contact us.

Based on the participants in my networking seminars, it seems many people just aren't sure exactly how to effectively follow up. Perhaps this is why so many people say, "Well, I tried networking but it's just a waste of time. It never turns into anything."

 Quick Quiz: Make a list of the business and social networking follow-up activities you participated in over the past three months. Were you persistent? Were you patient? Were you consistent? What were the most useful activities? Which were the least useful? Did you plan your follow-up? Are follow-up activities part of your regular routine?

Rules of Networking

To be effective, there are seven simple rules for networking that you should follow. These concepts are fundamental to follow-up success.

Rule #1: Invest Before You Withdraw

Networking, particularly in the beginning, is about willingness to give without measuring or keeping score. It's not about what you can get from other people. It's not about extraction. A big mistake that many people make is waiting until they need something to contact people in their network.

However, before you can withdraw from your resources, you

first need to have invested by making deposits. Think about it: Who would you rather be approached by, Mark or Clark?

> MARK: "I just got laid off and I'm wondering if you know of any opportunities to help me?"
> CLARK: "What can I do to help you become more successful?"

If you wait to approach someone when you're in need, it seems as if you are only interested in helping yourself. It's the business form of begging. In fact, I think that's why most people find networking so uncomfortable: they feel as though they are asking for a handout. Instead, if you invest early and approach networking with the idea of genuinely wanting to help the other person, think how much more receptive the other party would be and how much more comfortable you would be asking for something in the future.

When you invest in interactions over time, when you give without expectation, your actions earn trust. Then, when you need to eventually make a withdrawal, others will want to return the favor. Most people enjoy helping those who have helped them in the past.

Rule #2: Pay It Forward

However, sometimes it's not those that we help that return the favor. Those you have directly helped may not be able to assist you. That's why I recommend that your follow-up activities be based on the concept of pay it forward. Add value and ask for nothing in return. Although value is in the eye of the beholder, in general value comes in the form of money, information, connections, or time.

Interestingly, Benjamin Franklin was the original inventor and practitioner of pay it forward. He described it as a "trick [. . .] for doing a deal of good with a little money." The main idea is that a favor is not repaid directly to you, but rather to someone else. For example, while I was interviewing Guy Kawasaki about the strategies he used to propel his book *Enchantment* to the bestseller list, he mentioned that Dr. Robert Cialdini (author of the bestseller

Influence) promoted Guy's book from his Web site. Robert Cialdini was doing a favor for Guy. Guy then offered to do the same thing for my book on his Web site. So in essence, he was paying back the favor he received from Robert to me. He called it "karma" but the idea is the same.

Help others without any expectation that the favor will be returned directly to you. Use initial conversations to figure out how to best use your talents to serve your conversation partners. Then give freely, without expectation. The better you get at this, the easier follow-up becomes.

Rule #3: Don't Procrastinate

Most people have good intentions. After initial contact, we intend to follow up, but when we return to our work and personal lives we never seem to get around to it. Instead we attend to the issues that bubbled up while we were away and networking activity moves down our list of priorities. Or worse, we schedule time for follow-up, but feel like we don't have anything significant to share or don't have any specific next steps in mind, so we postpone our follow-up communication for another day. The problem is that when you postpone communication, relationships suffer.

So even if it's a short e-mail ("Hi, how are you? Hope that project you were working on is going well"), make it a point to reach out to your contact and don't postpone.

Rule #4: Be Consistent

Consistency is crucial. You want people who receive your follow-up to be able to count on you. With consistency, your network will begin to look forward to your regular follow-up. Create rules for yourself; some in your network will get three-month follow-ups, some six, other more, other less.

If you promise to contact someone in two weeks, then be sure to do so. If they suggest you wait six months, then follow up in six months.

Being consistent with your follow-up applies to you as well.

Establish benchmarks for yourself. For example: Set one hour aside every Friday afternoon for making networking phone calls; thirty minutes every day to tending your social media channels; and complete two major projects per month. Consistency will create better results.

Rule #5: Be Persistent, but Patient

In addition to consistency, repetition is also important. It's through repetition that you establish your credibility and familiarity. It's repetition that causes you or your company to be considered first when a need for your product or service arises. Don't assume that just because you sent something or posted something, your intended receiver saw it and will remember it. When you haven't heard from someone, don't assume they received your information and didn't find it helpful or lost interest. Remember: People have busy lives and full inboxes. Your communication may have simply gotten lost in the shuffle. You need to keep following up until you receive a definitive response. Only based on the response will you then determine the best way to continue your follow-up. Repetition is the key to successful networking.

 Warning: There's a fine line between pestering and checking in. This means you need to be careful that your communication is not perceived as spam. It's normal for people's priorities and interests to ebb and flow. It's best to ask, "When should I follow up next?" or "Are you open to more information?" Delivering unwanted communication is damaging to the relationship.

Rule #6: Advance the Conversation

When you create your follow-up, always be sure to invite further interaction. One way to do that is by asking questions. Questions make it easy for people to respond and will increase the number of interactions you have. At times, the topic isn't nearly as important as simply asking something so that the conversation advances another step.

Another great way to encourage a response is to invite feedback. When you ask someone's opinion, you are demonstrating your respect for them. For example, I encourage my clients to ask for feedback on their presentations. I suggest asking for one specific thing done well and one thing for improvement. By asking for one of each, they are much more likely to get useful feedback, instead of "Oh, yes, we like it." By asking for feedback you are giving your conversation partner an opportunity to provide you value while also advancing the conversation. See chapter 6 for more on feedback.

Rule #7: Plan Your Follow-Up

If you want to further develop relationships with the right people, then you need to hang out where those people hang out. Of course, you need to know who the right people are to begin with. Be sure you are clear about who might be able to potentially help you achieve what you want in life and make a plan for deepening your connection with those select people. Be creative with your plan. Select events that may attract the people you want to get to know and mark your calendar. It could be business events, social events, or cultural events. Make sure you plan in advance how you can help the people who will be attending the event and if possible, set-up in advance a time to meet with them during the event.

How Can You Put These Rules to Work?

Now that I've covered the seven fundamental follow-up rules, the next step is to create your networking plan based on the rules. How often will you follow up? With whom will you follow up? And finally, how will you follow up? Read the tips below to give you some practical ideas of how to put the rules into action.

Tip #1: Send Follow-Up E-mails

Currently, Facebook, Twitter, and SMS texting are the more popular tools for personal communication, but when it comes to professional networking, e-mail is more common. Tools will come and go, but what remains crucial for networking is brief, casual communication.

It's very common for me to send an e-mail that says, "Just checking in. How's it going?" or "We haven't talked in a while. Just wondering how you're doing," or "Thinking of you. Got any good news to share?" I've found that if you send a short note like this, you are very likely to receive a response. It may not be immediate, but it's likely you will eventually hear back.

If you have more time or the connection is strategic, you might want to check out the contact's social media profiles or blogs to see what's new. Did he change jobs? Did she win an award? Did he enter a contest that you can vote in? You can add a comment about whatever news you found.

On the flip side, some people like to send out quarterly/monthly/weekly e-mail updates. This might work well for people in your network that you have limited interaction with. However, I'm not a big fan of e-mail newsletters because they seem too impersonal. But if yours is well written or includes excellent content, that's certainly an option.

For example, I enjoy getting updates from Chris Brogan. His updates tend to be relatively short and written in a conversational style. I also enjoy getting Christopher S. Penn's "Out of Date" newsletter because he condenses about a month's worth of valuable information into one e-mail. However, I won't call out the many newsletters that go directly into my spam folder! For this type of communication, the adage "Content is King" still rings true.

Tip #2: Personalize Outgoing Social Media Connection Requests

When you send social media connection requests, be sure to personalize them. I like to remind the receiver how we initially connected and if possible, I like to include a brief compliment and a short question. The easiest thing to do is to ask a question or two that the person can easily respond to. I always hope the person will not only respond to my question(s) but also include a few follow-up questions for me, to keep the conversation moving forward.

Here are a few examples of what I've written:

- "I really enjoy your blog. What's been your most challenging/popular/interesting topic so far?"
- "It was great to meet you at the conference. I really enjoyed our conversation about engagement. It would be good to connect here so we can keep in touch. What are you working on now?"
- "Hope you'll accept my connection. I really enjoyed the conference and particularly your session. It was inspiring. Which session did you enjoy the most?"

With new contacts, your goal is to search for common ground. Review online profiles to see if there is anything in common, whether it's a contact, a school, or an interest. Use that information to create further conversation.

Tip #3: Respond to Incoming Connections Requests

In my case, because of my Public Speaker podcast and because I talk to large groups, I often get social media connection requests from people who are familiar with me, but who I don't know personally. I always accept all incoming requests and respond to the request with a short message.

If a connection invitation comes from someone who seems like a good potential alliance, I try to extend and deepen the initial connection by learning a bit more about the person before I send back my reply. I'll often check out their profile, maybe visit their Web page, or read some of their work.

In general, I try to thank them for contacting me, give some information, and perhaps ask a question. That way it moves the conversation forward. If they reply to my message (which often happens), then I get to know that person a little bit better. I've had many opportunities unfold as a result of these short message follow-ups.

Tip #4: Pick Up the Phone or Schedule a Video Conference

While the above methods are good, if I am interested in deepening a connection more quickly, or renewing a connection that seems to have withered, I'll schedule a phone or video conference call. I prefer video because then I can see the person and feel like the interaction is more personal. I like to simply talk and joke with someone in person—I believe it allows me to get to know them more naturally. This of course requires schedule coordination and needs to be planned in advance. However, a direct one-on-one conversation can quickly move a relationship forward or rekindle a relationship that might be in need of a boost. Never worry that it's been too long since you last talked with someone. Most people are so busy that they are happy to reconnect no matter how much time has passed.

Tip #5: Plan an Interesting In-Person Meeting

When I was a teenager, I dreamed of holding a Third Period World History Study Group at the public pool. I spent much time trying to convince my parents that as the spring heated up, I would be much better able to study for finals if I were cooler, tanner, and with my friends who shared a pressing need to be cooler, tanner, and deepen their understanding of the significance of the Middle Ages by Monday. Oddly enough, my parents never shared my vision.

As an adult, of course, I realize that my A in class was thanks, in part, to my parents who saw a bad idea and kept me from it. The other thing I realized as an adult, though, is that, in theory, I actually had a great idea. People do this successfully and effectively in professional situations all the time.

One of the best ways to deepen connections is to spend time with someone. Of course, this is the reason why so much business happens at ball games and on golf courses. I like to attend conferences in which other attendees are people I'd like to spend time with. I make an effort to schedule my day so that I end up sitting either at a meal or during a session with someone that I'd like to know better.

If the person is local, then I try to tag along on an activity that the person is already doing. For example, if the other person is a runner and you are a runner, you might suggest taking a run together. For people who have very busy schedules, this is a particularly effective way to get some face time.

However, before you request an in-person meeting, consider if it's absolutely necessary. Simply asking to "pick your brain" or "get to know each other" is often not specific enough. It's important to have clear and specific goals for the meeting before you engage someone's time.

 Warning: If you need to ask a favor, especially of a successful person, it is best to directly ask the favor ahead of time, instead of obfuscating your request. It may seem somewhat rude, but successful people value time. Be as specific as possible, and most will know almost immediately if they can help or not. No pretense needed.

Tip #6: Engage with Blogs and Other Social Media

To increase your interactions, comment on other people's social media channels. Engage on a few different sites (Google+, Facebook, Twitter, YouTube, etc.) so that your name and face become more familiar. Choose people that could be strategic to your success and also search for people who are actively engaging in your topic area. If the person you are trying to reach out to has a blog, then read it, actively comment, and participate in his/her online community. Always be careful to maintain thoughtful, intelligent interaction, not just interaction for interaction's sake.

For example, entrepreneur and wine expert Gary Vaynerchuk initially started engaging with anyone who was talking about wine.

He offered his expert advice and opinions free of charge. Because he followed all the rules of follow-up with energy and enthusiasm, today his name is a recognizable brand and it's likely he can contact anyone (including celebrities, hard to reach media, or even politicians) through social media and get an almost immediate response.

Tip #7: Send Resources That Might Be Helpful

Always keep tucked away in your mind the kinds of information that your network would find valuable. Then, when you are engaged in your normal daily activities, when you read or hear something interesting or useful, think "Who else might benefit from this information?" Then either share in that moment or mark it for networking material. They key is to always be thinking "Who else can benefit from this?" When I find a valuable resource, I try to share it directly with at least three people in my network. If it's something directly related to my specific topics in "workplace communication" then I also try to share it as a status update on my social networks.

For example, my fellow Quick and Dirty Tips podcast host, Get-It-Done Guy (aka Stever Robbins) attended a conference on social media a little while back. Throughout the weekend, as he learned valuable information, he sent e-mails to me and some other fellow Quick and Dirty Tips hosts who he thought would find it useful. And you know what? We did!

One of my clients attended a conference and composed Twitter messages throughout the event. He ended up not only engaging the staff who couldn't attend, but his tweets also got noticed by media professionals attending the event—so much so that they sought him out. As a by-product of one of the meetings, his work was featured in a major journal.

I love to be on the receiving end of helpful resources, especially when the sender points out why the information would be helpful to me. However, just writing "thought you might enjoy this" or "thought you might find this useful" is not enough. I want the sender to take the extra step to explain to me why I should read it so that I can quickly prioritize the message.

Tip #8: Monitor Your Network Activities and Offer Your Help

One follow-up activity that is important, and often overlooked, is monitoring your network and listening to what is going on around you. Not only should you be closely following your primary connections, you should also be listening to what the movers and shakers of your industry are talking about. Monitoring is important so that you can be aware, or better anticipate, what help people in your network might need. When it's clear that you might be able to help, communicate what you can do for them in a sincere manner. Offer your assistance and then deliver. Ensure that what you provide is of the highest quality.

For example, I might offer to help connect people in my network. I might review a book or a blog. I might offer encouragement. I might offer some advice or make a recommendation or referral. I might even offer to speak at an event. We all have talents and a sincere offer of your assistance can go a long way toward building a relationship.

Recently, I heard Garr Reynolds give a speech and at the end he requested some information from the audience. Since Garr had been on my list of "want to meet" people, I jumped on the opportunity to help him with his request. That evening, I briefly introduced myself and offered my assistance. I also made an effort to share common ground with him. From reading his blog, I knew he had a young daughter about the age of my young daughters. My goal in the very first communication was to connect on a professional and personal level, while at the same time offering my help, if he wanted it.

He responded by making a comment about his daughter and requesting to see some of my work. When I got home, I sent him general video and audio of my work and also offered to send him a presentation relating to his specific request. I purposefully chose NOT to send him the specifics of his request in the first few interactions. I wanted to build credibility and trust before I sent him exactly what he was requesting. I wanted to develop a deeper connection first.

Tip #9: Use Mutual Connections to Boost Credibility

By the way, I also included in my initial communication to Garr a reference to a conversation that I had had with Guy Kawasaki. I knew that Garr knew and respected Guy so I was hoping our mutual contact would help to strengthen our initial connection.

It's even better if your mutual connection is willing to recommend you and your services. It's commonly labeled referral marketing, but if you think about it, it's the way most of us make purchases today. We ask our friends for a reference, or we go to a shopping site and read the reviews, or we look to our social media network for recommendations. Professional networking is no different in this regard.

Tip #10: Give Referrals

Write a recommendation for someone's product or service and submit it to a variety of relevant sites. For example, you could refer someone in your network to someone else in your network. You could refer someone by writing them a recommendation on their professional networking site (e.g. LinkedIn or Xing). You could write a short post either on Facebook, Google+, your blog or newsletter talking about your experience with a person, product, or service. You could write a positive public review of a product (e.g., a book, a toaster, an online course) on a shopping site. Keep in mind that when you refer people to others in your network, you are helping and deepening two relationships at the same time.

Tip #11: Celebrate Achievements

Another easy way to deepen connections is to celebrate achievements—theirs or yours. Let's say I notice that someone got a research grant, or they got a new job, or I hear they finally sold their house. I'll send a quick, "Congratulations, way to go!" message.

Occasionally, if something good happens to me, I might send an e-mail that says, "Just a quick update. I'm excited because I just got an article published. Any good news on your end?" In a way, my message gives my connections the permission to brag a bit. And I enjoy reading the responses because it allows me to get to know what is important to that particular person.

Tip #12: Contact Someone You Haven't Been in Touch with for a Long Time

When we move on to a new job, it's tempting to leave those work friendships behind. But if it's reasonably possible, try to occasionally touch base with your former colleagues via e-mail or social media. For someone I haven't contacted in a long time, I just say, "Hey, just wondering what you've been up to since I last talked with you. I'd love to hear from you when you have time."

When leaving former positions, hopefully you didn't burn any bridges. That means that you are still on friendly, though maybe not frequent, terms. Why not get together with your former boss and see how he/she is doing? You never know what you can learn or what that can lead to.

Tip #13: Request a "Lunch and Learn"

A "lunch and learn" is just a meeting designed to share knowledge with a group while the participants are eating lunch. This creates an opportunity for employees to extend and build connections within organizations. Depending on the topic, you may be able to attract attendees who don't normally interact with each other. The event itself provides a comfortable format for people to build new connections as well as an opportunity for employees to further their professional development, which in turn, further strengthens their relationship with the company. In fact, several of my clients have told me that they love my lunch and learn programs for exactly those reasons.

Check This Out: Would you like for me to come to your workplace for a lunch and learn program? Visit www .smarttalksuccess.com/lunchwithlisa to nominate your company for a free event.

However, this concept can also be applied to a one-on-one lunch meeting. We often fall into the rut of having lunch with the same people every day or every week. Or worse, we eat alone at our desks. Branch out of your department and get to know some other employees of your company. Better yet, once a month schedule a lunch with experts from your industry. Typically this type of "lunch and learn" is about social networking. No experts in your local area? Work from home? No problem, schedule a video or telephone conference. Sharing a meal with someone is an excellent way to build trust and teamwork, plus it's efficient. You were going to eat anyway.

Tip #14: Participate in Professional Organizations

Many industries have organizations that meet regularly for training and connecting (and, sometimes, commiserating!). Find an organization that supports your career goals, or consider joining one. For example, you could try Toastmasters, which is an organization to help public speakers, or the IAAP, the International Association of Administrative Professionals. Neither organization targets just one industry, but instead supports anyone who practices particular skills in their jobs and life.

Tip #15: Attend Alumni Events

If you graduated from college, chances are your school regularly hosts alumni events. This is a great way to reconnect with former classmates or others who shared a similar college experience but may be in a different field than you are. Don't be a stranger to your alma mater!

Tip #16: Speak at Events

If you have a particular skill or area of expertise, offer to speak to professional organizations, civic groups, church groups, or schools. Even if the group is small, you can make lasting connections and keep yourself in their mind as a possible contact. Contact your chamber of commerce or register with online speaker sites to offer your availability, or keep watch for topics that groups may be interested in booking you for events.

If solo public speaking isn't your thing, consider joining a panel. As you build your network, you may be able to supply several of the panel members for an organization that is just starting out.

VIP Bonus: At this point you may be thinking, "Lisa, these activities are time consuming!" The key is to use technology to help make the process fast and efficient. There's software for pasting snippets of text, there's software for managing contacts and reminders for follow-up, there's software for managing business cards and contact information, there's software for monitoring and managing social media, and there are Web sites for posting your availability as a speaker. There is no way I could effectively and efficiently follow up if it weren't for many of these tools. Visit www.smarttalksuccess.com/vip for a list of my favorites.

Tip #17: Write Articles, Books, or Podcasts

Submit articles to professional publications. Write a blog using your knowledge. Share tips on social media or perhaps even write a book. Become known as a "go-to" person who offers great advice and content in your particular field.

For example, in December 2011, twenty-nine-year-old Clara Shih was chosen to join Starbucks' board of directors. How did she get there? Obviously she's smart, but so are many other people. One thing that made her stand out was that while working in marketing and alliances at salesforce.com she wrote a book, *The Facebook Era,* which went on to become a bestseller. Because of her book, she was able to gain exposure, which led to numerous opportunities for her. Although her book was published by a major publisher, today it's easier than ever to write and self-publish a book that allows you to reach and serve a much larger network of professionals. I firmly believe that we all have a story to tell and ideas to share. Think about what you can share and start writing.

Tip #18: Buy Someone's Product or Service

Rather read than write? Buy copies of someone's book in your network and give them out as gifts to other people in your network who you think would find that book useful. Inscribe each book with a personalized message and every time the book is opened, the receiver will be reminded of you.

Attend a conference or a speaking event of someone you'd like to meet. By paying money for someone's product or service you are showing (with actions rather than just words) that you support or believe in them and their product.

Tip #19: Send Real Mail

Send handwritten letters of appreciation. Yes, break out the stationary and write a quick note. (Quick, before the U.S. Postal Service goes completely out of business!) There's something wonderful about receiving a handwritten letter. In my business, I've started sending out handwritten thank-you cards because they leave a much stronger, more lasting impression.

Tip #20: Wait

This may sound odd, but my final follow-up technique is to wait. I'm not saying procrastinate. What I'm suggesting is that at times, it's best to move slowly and build your interaction over time. The best follow-up might be to schedule your follow-up for a later date. Without enough time between follow-ups you might run the risk of being perceived as pesky or intrusive and sour the relationship. People need adequate time to digest and process information. To avoid this problem, ask when and how your contact would like you to follow up.

Summary: How to Effectively Follow Up Your Conversations

✓ Follow-up is what builds and strengthens relationships.
✓ Persistent, consistent, and patient follow-up is critical to advance a relationship.
✓ Invest in building and strengthening your network before you begin to make withdrawals.
✓ Add value and ask (and expect) nothing in return.
✓ Don't postpone or procrastinate. There is always a way to follow up.
✓ Be consistent so others will begin to count on you.
✓ Be persistent, but patient. Repetition helps others to keep you top of mind.
✓ Advance your conversations by asking questions.
✓ Plan your follow-up so you expand your network purposefully.
✓ 20 Ways to Follow up:
  ▸ Send e-mails.
  ▸ Personalize outgoing social media requests.
  ▸ Respond to incoming connections request.
  ▸ Schedule telephone and video conferences.
  ▸ Plan an in-person meeting.
  ▸ Engage with blogs and other social media.
  ▸ Send resources that might be helpful.
  ▸ Monitor your connections activities and offer help.
  ▸ Use mutual connections to boost your credibility.
  ▸ Give referrals.
  ▸ Celebrate achievements.
  ▸ Contact someone you've lost touch with.
  ▸ Request a "lunch and learn."
  ▸ Participate in professional organizations.
  ▸ Attend alumni events.

- ▸ Speak at events.
- ▸ Write articles, books, or podcasts.
- ▸ Buy someone's product or services.
- ▸ Send real mail.
- ▸ Wait.

Smart Talk Challenge #1:
Choose one person in your personal or professional network and reach out to them right now. Choose a method of follow-up that you've never tried before. Go ahead. What are you waiting for?

Smart Talk Challenge #2:
Choose the three most valuable contacts in your current network and think about what you could do to improve the relationship. Plan the "what" and "when" of your follow-up for these main contacts right now. Plan at least three follow-up activities for each. Put the activities into your calendar right now.

Smart Talk Challenge #3:
Think about a topic that your prospects would find valuable. Write a 500-word article on the topic. Don't have writing skills? Hire someone to ghostwrite it for you. Send this article to the appropriate contacts in your network.

Case Study: Mac Smith

"In 2005, I had just finished my Masters degree and was starting on my Ph.D. During the annual career conference at my university, different companies come out to show what they do. During that year, I met researchers and gaming students who had the same background as me. I didn't even realize that people from my profession could get into video games. I was still three years away from being on the job market, but I knew this was something I was passionate about. At that conference, I realized any job working in video games was cool but I also realized by looking at the number people at the booth just how competitive it was.

"So, I started off by meeting the lead manager at that conference. I had a 'get to know you' interview and told him, 'I'm not going to be on the market for a very long time, but I'm very interested in what you do. I want to know more about what I can do to put myself in a good position for when I do get out.' I made sure to let him know I was going to stay in touch with him. He agreed and I e-mailed him directly after the conference. My first e-mail, was simply restating my interest in keeping in touch. He responded by saying, 'That's great.'

"I waited about four months and followed up again. It was under the guise of an internship. I'd say, 'Just following up to see if you are going to have any internships available this fall, and if not, here's the really cool stuff I've been working on.' I'd attach papers or work that I'd done along with a link to my student Web page. I did this every four to six months, just so that he would remember who I was. I also did this for ten or fifteen other people in the video game field who I was interested in.

"In my last year of school, I started to get serious with my job search. I thought, 'OK, I established who I am. Have I really established why I'm a better fit than any other candidate?' My skill set was good but someone could top my video game specific experience with more direct experience in gaming. So over the course of the last year I worked on small side projects that applied to gaming. Then I started to publish some game space research results and sending that to Microsoft with a bit more frequency [every month or two]. I eventually asked them if I might be able to help them by doing a small project for them. So over my last year in school, I created this really robust story, not only about who I was but also by having these really specific examples of how I could help that team at Microsoft in ways that nobody else could.

"About six months before I was to graduate, I started sending more directive e-mails: 'I'll be graduating in six months and I'd really like to work with you. Please keep me in mind.' Then, every month, I kept sending updates on my work and letting them know exactly when I was going to be available. I also created a new Web site with all my projects.

"Unfortunately, when I got out, they didn't have any positions available. But they called me and said, 'We don't have anything right now, but we're really interested. Keep talking with us.' About seven months later, they called for an interview and my Web site got a big number of hits. I could see what they were interested in me by looking at my page statistics.

"All the years of preparation leading up to this interview took the pressure off because they knew the quality of my work. The most powerful thing about communicating with the company for such a long period of time was that I learned what was important to them. I could present myself in a way that I knew would be attractive to them. Ultimately, I was offered and accepted a position with them. It was just over three years later that I got hired by the same guy that I first interviewed with at the original conference."

💬 💬 💬

There were more than 10,000 applicants for that one position. So as you can see, persistent, consistent communication pays off! A few years later, Mac Smith was recruited by Google, where he currently works as a researcher.

VIP Bonus: Download the full audio interview and get other exclusive information and benefits by joining my free members-only VIP site: www.smarttalksuccess.com/VIP.

5. From Archie Bunker to Mary Poppins: How to Speak with Tact and Grace

Just a spoonful of sugar helps the medicine go down.

—"A Spoonful of Sugar," performed by Julie Andrews

Imagine that you're trying to generate new business from existing clients. You've been on the phone all afternoon, connecting, talking about last night's game and upcoming weekend plans. A coworker of yours walks by and clearly overhears your conversations that, from his perspective, sound like personal calls.

Now imagine that you're having lunch with that same coworker and your boss. During your conversation, your boss tells you that she appreciates the work you did on a recent project. Your coworker chimes in saying, albeit playfully, "Oh, yeah, she's a great worker—when she's not wasting time talking on the phone!" clearly implying that you spend too much time on personal business and not enough time on your job.

Your coworker doesn't realize that you've been building, strengthening, and deepening relationships with your clients for the betterment of your company. However, this isn't the first time this coworker has made a snarky comment. In fact, he has done it several times, both publicly and privately.

Maybe the coworker was just playing around. Maybe it came from jealousy, maybe it came from ambition, or maybe he just doesn't like you. Whatever the case, your coworker just told your boss that you're not doing your job. He suggested that you're wasting company time on personal business.

So how do you handle the situation? How do educate your coworker and boss on the situation while still maintaining a positive relationship with both?

 Quick Quiz: When was the last time you were put into an awkward situation by someone else? Did you feel your only options were to take it on the chin, or risk hurting their feelings or reputation?

Author and critic Isaac Goldberg said, "Diplomacy is to do and say, The nastiest thing in the nicest way." I prefer to put it this way: Diplomacy is the ability to tell someone something that is difficult to hear and have them thank you for it. In other words, remember that no one likes to be called an idiot.

For me, *business* diplomacy means achieving goals by sharing information and ideas in a helpful, positive way. It's the difference between tying a note to a brick and throwing it through the window or sending a polite, nicely written letter on fancy, scented stationary. The message may be the same, but the delivery method is completely different. When it comes to diplomacy, it's all in the delivery.

In business, diplomacy is the key to successful relationships. Business diplomacy is the art of expressing your thoughts, opinions, and ideas in ways that do not offend or put off others. In short, diplomacy is putting into practice the idea of "it's not what you say, but how you say it."

Why Is Diplomacy So Important?

The end goal of business communication is to affect change. Think about it. Even in sales, you are ultimately trying to get someone to change their behavior by getting them to purchase your product or service. The problem is, when we tell people they need to change, we're also telling them, by implication, that they're doing something wrong!

People often like to compare business with war, especially when talking about negotiations and diplomacy. In the political arena, the consequences of war over diplomacy are real and tangible. Everyone understands what happens when diplomacy fails, and so its importance can't be understated.

In the business arena, though, the consequences of failing to be diplomatic aren't always so obvious. We don't recognize them as readily, though they are no less real. Good business requires good relationships, even with competitors. Without diplomacy, good relationships can go bad. Fast.

You have to interact with people at work every day. You're probably in constant communication with your boss, with your subordinates and with your coworkers. All of you have your own idiosyncrasies and your own way of doing things.

Sometimes, you may have to deal with a problem employee or a difficult boss. You need to learn how to let them know their actions are hurting the work environment or productivity. You also have to preserve your working relationship. Using business diplomacy is the only way to convey your feelings and to affect change.

It's vital, then, to understand not only the importance of building relationships, but of maintaining them. That's when diplomacy is most important. When people believe that you have their best interests at heart, they are far more likely to want to work with you. When we use tact and grace, we build trust. When we use words and tactics that hurt, we burn bridges and lose clients.

Quick Quiz: Have you ever had a relationship go sour because you weren't diplomatic? What do you think you could have said or done differently?

How Do I Use Diplomacy in Business?

In politics, examples of diplomacy are everywhere. For example, neighboring countries India and Pakistan are bitter rivals. They've existed in a state of conflict more or less since they were partitioned in 1947. In early 2011 peace talks between the two nations had been stalled for nearly a year.

At the 2011 Cricket World Cup semifinals, the two rival nations found their teams playing head-to-head. The Indian prime minister, Manmohan Singh, shocked the world when he graciously invited his Pakistani counterpart to watch the match with him. The move provided the spark needed to revive negotiations between the two countries and showed that the Indian prime minister was a man not only of words, but of action.

In business, the end goals may be different, but the principles are the same. Becoming a diplomatic communicator means using reason, kindness and compassion. People have to believe that you are working for them, not against them. Just as the Indian prime minister demonstrated with his gesture to Pakistan, diplomats show respect for the other person in their business dealings.

Diplomatic communications demonstrate that you understand and validate the other person's thoughts, feelings or ideas. At the same time, you gently present your side of the argument. A diplomatic communicator is someone who can get their message across and convince people to change without damaging the relationship. This quote sums it nicely: "Diplomacy is the business of handling a porcupine without disturbing the quills."

As in all relationships, diplomatic communications require honesty. In fact, there's no need for diplomacy without honesty. So when practicing diplomacy, you must be honest—just not brutally honest! This doesn't mean you should misrepresent the truth, it simply means that at the end of the communication the other person should feel positive about the relationship. They should leave the negotiating table feeling respected, not dejected.

 Warning: Diplomacy doesn't mean you need to compromise your position. You can still stand firm on issues that you believe in, but make sure your points are expressed politely and respectfully, while at the same time taking into consideration the other party's need to be validated.

Three Rules for Dealing with People Diplomatically

To be an effective business diplomat, there are three simple rules that you should follow. These concepts are fundamental to dealing with people. You may find that they're not just good advice for business, but they're also basic rules for being a decent human being! These rules were heavily influenced by Dale Carnegie's famous book *How to Win Friends and Influence People*.

#1 Rule of Diplomacy: Don't Criticize

Carnegie says, "Criticism is futile because it puts a person on the defensive and usually makes him strive to justify himself. Criticism is dangerous, because it wounds a man's precious pride, hurts his sense of importance, and arouses resentment."

Think of the example at the beginning of this chapter. In that instance, you imagined a scenario in which you were put on the defensive by a coworker. Think about the emotions you would feel if a similar scenario happened to you in real life. You would likely feel like your hard work was unappreciated, and because the comment was made in front of your boss, your pride would no doubt be hurt and perhaps you might even feel angry.

In one sense, all of the hard work and time you put into building the relationship with your client was invalidated by one snarky comment by a coworker. You would probably resent not only the remark, but the coworker, as well. The two of you would be far less likely to be productive when working together on future projects.

Carnegie's statement holds true not only for criticism of others, but for self-criticism, also. Don't get down on yourself or others. Negative criticism makes people feel bad, and is not effective.

Let me emphasize that last point. Your goal is to identify areas for improvement. So when you see something that is wrong, don't just point at the flaw, but also suggest constructive ways to fix the flaw. In fact, don't even call it a flaw. Try saying something along the lines of "Hey, I noticed you were doing it this way, but have you ever thought about trying another tactic? You might find it easier and more efficient."

Be positive, not negative. Work to build up, not tear down. Don't present a problem without solutions. And yes, that's solutions— plural! If and when it's possible, you should always provide alternatives. That way, the person on the receiving end will still feel like they are in control and ultimately gets to make the final decision.

Remember the old saying, "You can catch more flies with honey than vinegar." People are far more likely to respond to gentle persuasion than heavy-handed tactics, and in the end you'll be far more respected and appreciated. By offering solutions instead of just pointing out problems, people will believe that you honestly care about them and work with you.

#2 Rule of Diplomacy: Be Appreciative

No one likes it when their work is rejected, and oftentimes they take it personally. Everyone, however, likes to feel appreciated. Even when you have to reject an idea, your rejection should come with appreciation for the work that was put into it.

 Warning: Don't lay it on thick with false flattery. People will see through that in an instant, and your praise will be recognized for what it is: meaningless. Appreciation should be honest and sincere.

Expressing appreciation can be as simple as saying "Thanks." Appreciation should be expressed frequently in order to maintain a positive atmosphere. It should be both public and private in order to carry the most weight. Public to give people the recognition they deserve, and private to convey the sincerity that true appreciation requires.

I'll never forget a boss I once had—my boss's boss, actually—who I consider to this day to be the king of appreciation. Fred Dewey was his name, and I remember him regularly sending short and sincere "way-to-go" e-mails. He was always quick to notice and appreciate hard work and extra effort, and made it a point to include all of the right people on the e-mail so bosses and colleagues saw you receive the recognition as well.

Fred's e-mails only cost him a minute to write, but they had a tremendous payoff in the long run. His minor investment resulted in major boosts in productivity and personal political capital. His frequent, consistent praise, both public and private, fueled my confidence and earned my deepest respect. Moreover, and probably more important to the company's bottom line (we are, after all, talking business), Fred motivated me to work even harder and be even more productive. I know this was true for my colleagues as well.

Everyone at work loved Fred. So when he asked someone to go the extra mile on a task or a project, or do something that wasn't in their job description, do you think they ever told him no? Of course not!

Likewise, because Fred was always so quick to express his appreciation, on the occasions when he offered alternative solutions to challenges or presented a new or better way of doing things, do you think it was taken as criticism? Not at all. We believed Fred genuinely wanted the best, both for us and the company. Because he made it a point to let us know he believed in us, we made it a point to go above and beyond for him.

Appreciation is at the core of diplomatic communication. Remember, at times you may need to express your appreciation for what someone has done, said, or given while not agreeing with or liking it. Secretary of State Hillary Clinton, during a radio interview with a comedy duo, demonstrated how to express appreciation even when faced with an unappealing gift. The comedy team handed her a two-year-old bag of potato chips as a "gift." She responded, "I cannot tell you how much this means to me. I am an eater of chips." She went on to say, "There's a whole course on how to [express appreciation]."

The bottom line is this: appreciation costs you next to nothing to give, and it pays off dividends in the long run. Giving appreciation when due will take you a long way toward working effectively with other people.

#3 Rule of Diplomacy: See the Other Person's Point of View
Henry Ford said, "If there is any one secret of success, it lies in the ability to get the other person's point of view and see things from that person's angle as well as from your own."

When you take the time to put yourself in the other person's shoes, you get a new perspective that you may not have had before. You'll gain the ability to see a bigger part of the picture, and you'll get a look at the problem from another angle. You'll also get a better feel for the kind of solution they need, and not just the one you want.

By getting the perspective of the other person, you'll be better able to show genuine concern. I can't understate the importance of this. When you demonstrate that you care about other people's thoughts and feelings, they will believe that you're making an effort to listen and understand their position. In most cases, people just want to feel like they've been heard.

How Can You Put These Rules to Work?

When I first developed these rules, I wasn't exactly sure how to implement them on a practical level. "How do you do this at work? How exactly do you avoid being critical? What's the best way to show appreciation? And how on Earth do you learn to see things from another person's point of view?"

I've already told you that a key concept of diplomacy lies in the old phrase, "It's not what you say; it's how you say it." The best way to actually say something diplomatically may not always be so obvious. To help you put my rules of business diplomacy into practice, I've come up with five tips.

Tip #1: Be Observant and Know the Players

As Sun Tzu said, in *The Art of War,* "Keep your friends close and your enemies closer." A business diplomat makes an effort to observe and understand the people they work with.

Do the same with your associates. What makes them tick? What is their typical communication style? How do they communicate with their body? What is their conflict resolution style? What are their interests? How do they approach problems? What is their cultural background? By knowing this information you can address their needs in a way that is comfortable to them.

Tip #2: Learn to Flex Your Communication Style

People communicate differently—not worse, not better, just differently. Many young professionals make the mistake of thinking that their own communication style is the best (or only) way to communicate. Diplomatic communicators recognize other people's preferred communication styles and flex theirs to accommodate.

Many authors[1,2,3] have defined behavioral and communication styles using a variety of terms. Based on these, I created my own terminology because I found it easier to be able to remember and quickly profile someone while speaking with them. You can use this as a tool to help you to rapidly build relationships by adjusting your communication style to that of your partner:

The Scientific Approach

A person who communicates using the scientific approach prefers data and facts. Details and accuracy are very important. This person doesn't mind spending extra time to make sure things are right. When talking with this type of communicator it's best to be specific, accurate, neat, and tactful.

The Team Player Approach

A person who communicates using the team player approach prefers to focus on maintaining relationships and maintaining security. This person is often relaxed, deliberate, and doesn't seek the spotlight. When talking with a team player communicator, you need to be positive, patient, and personable. Be sure to schedule time to chat and recognize his or her achievements.

The Spirited Approach

A person who communicates using the spirited approach is outgoing, flamboyant, energetic, and spontaneous. When communicating with a spirited communicator, crank up your enthusiasm level to keep up with theirs. That way, your message will be delivered at their comfort level.

The Results-Only Approach

A person who communicates using the results-only approach is very direct, practical, demanding, and to the point. Many find this type of communicator to be brusque or "difficult." The key to connecting with results-only types is to be brief, prepared, organized, and confident.

🗨 🗨 🗨

Understanding your style and the styles of those around you will help you communicate effectively. However it's also important to recognize that we each use different styles at different times, although most of us have a preferred style for when we are under stress and a different preferred style when we are not under stress.

For example, let's say that, in general, you prefer the results-only approach and you need to provide information to someone who generally prefers the scientific approach. If you know that, you also know that it's important to slow down and take extra time to provide not just a summary, but to include all the details. Be sure to give someone who prefers this style enough time to think through the information before requesting a response from them.

Or let's say you prefer the spirited approach and you need to talk with someone who prefers the team player approach. You'll want to let him or her know ahead of time that you'd like to talk. Slow down and talk slightly quieter. Be sure to start the conversation by asking about relationships that are important to them.

Good communicators learn how to modify their communication style to better match the styles of others. By flexing your style, you can communicate more effectively with others, which leads to better results. To be clear, I'm not suggesting you change your personality, but rather temporarily modify your communication approach to best achieve your goals.

Throughout my career, I've had the pleasure of facilitating communication styles training for numerous teams. Having a model for understanding communication styles is an extremely valuable management tool, and goes a long way toward diplomatic business communication.

VIP Bonus: Learn more about your communication style. Visit www.smarttalksuccess.com/VIP to take a communication style quiz. **VIP**

Tip #3: Choose Your Words Carefully

We've already acknowledged that no one likes to have their work and ideas rejected. Unfortunately, there are times when we have to deliver bad news or we have to tell someone that we disagree with them. How do we accomplish this without leaving them feeling down and dejected?

Perhaps the most important element in using diplomacy is to choose your words carefully. Very carefully. My dad used to tell me, "Lisa, you don't have to say 'it's white' when instead you could say 'it's not black.'" What he was really telling me was that word choice is extremely important in forming and creating perceptions. Remember your mouth doesn't come with an eraser!

Politicians are, naturally, the most adept at this. Take domestic oil drilling, for example. Some politicians are more direct in calling it "drilling for oil." Others are far more euphemistic, calling it instead "energy exploration." Some will chide us for "not giving emergency care to undocumented workers," while others will advocate "denying health-care benefits to illegal aliens."

Different words, while they may mean the same thing, have different connotations. In his book *Words That Work,* political consultant and author Frank Luntz sums up the concept nicely when he says, "It's not what you say, it's what people hear."

When choosing the words you use, you have to consider more than what you think they mean. You must also think about how they will sound to other people. You can't just assume that people will automatically interpret something you said in the way you meant it.

It's also important to avoid phrases like "You have to . . .", "You always . . .", or "You never . . ." These can be viewed as aggressive. They are also generalities. Rarely is there such a thing as "always," "have to," or "never." Those are broad, sweeping words that leave no room for error. For every "always" you say, the other person will almost certainly be able to find an exception. This will not only turn them off to the rest of your message, but also diminish your credibility because they will likely be able to prove you wrong.

Instead, try using indirect language such as "You might consider . . .", "I think it might be stronger if . . .", or "It looks like . . ." Think about it. These phrases sound far less accusatory than "You always . . ." and they allow both you and the receiver far more wiggle room to work out any issues you may have.

Diplomatic communicators think, rethink, and then think some more about the words they choose before they communicate their ideas. They are fully aware that the wrong word in the wrong place to the wrong person can permanently damage a relationship or a reputation. The words you use are that important and that powerful.

Tip #4: Think and Be Open

As a new parent, I swore to myself I would never use the phrase "Because I said so, that's why!" when questioned by my children. Growing up, I couldn't stand hearing it from my parents. I'll bet you couldn't, either. You knew where you stood with your parents; you knew they were in charge. All you wanted to know was why. Hearing "because I said so" wasn't going to get the buy-in they needed to get you to listen to their point of view.

They same concept applies in business. I'll never forget my worst moment as a new manager. I once had an employee, Tom, who questioned why he needed to complete a task I assigned to him. In my frustration, I actually said to him, "You need to do it because I'm your manager and I told you to do it." The look on Tom's face is forever etched in my memory. Immediately, I realized my mistake. I hadn't been listening. I hadn't, up to that point, respected his needs, wants, and feelings, nor had I accepted that his viewpoint was different from mine.

Although I knew that I would achieve the short-term result that I wanted in getting him to complete his task, clearly I had severely damaged the relationship between us. I didn't take the time to consider his point of view or think about why I needed him to accomplish the task. I let my emotions get to me and I blurted out the first thought that came to my mind. Tom wasn't going to go the extra mile for me anytime in the near future. In fact, he was likely to resent the way I treated the situation and would be quietly passive aggressive in his dealings with me from that point on.

The lesson I took from that encounter was to listen, think, and be open. Diplomatic communicators consider their words very carefully before speaking. They remain in control of their emotions, and at all costs they avoid blurting out the first thing that comes to mind.

A diplomatic communicator consciously chooses when, how, and where to disagree. Diplomats also adhere to the mantra, "choose your battles" because the simple truth is: some things are worth fighting for, and some are not.

What happens, though, if you feel offended or angry? First things first, take a step back. I'm a big fan of deep breathing exercises. When situations arise that make me angry or offend me, I make it a point to say to myself, "Lisa, breathe. Just breathe." If that doesn't work, I'll suggest a short break so I can collect my thoughts and better plan what I want to say next.

After you've calmed down from your initial emotional reaction, take a moment to be as objective as possible. Try to look at things not only from the other person's point of view, but also as an unaffiliated, neutral outside observer. Assess the situation as objectively as possible and act accordingly, careful not to do or say anything you may regret later.

 Quick Quiz: Has anyone ever told you that you had to do something just because they held a position of authority over you? How did it make you feel? How did you react? Did you want to work for them again?

Tip #5: Relax Your Body and Your Face

Do you wear your emotions on your sleeve? Well, stop it! Being a diplomatic communicator means being able to appear relaxed, even when you're not. Humans are by and large visual creatures. We take in up to 90 percent of the information we receive through our eyes. Because of this, our body language is vital to diplomacy.

Your facial expressions, hand gestures, and posture communicate a tremendous amount about you and your thoughts, so it's important to be relaxed and calm and to maintain a conversational tone of voice. If you're a person who is known for having an expressive face, practice maintaining eye contact with a neutral, welcoming facial expression.

Relax any parts of your body that may become tense during difficult discussions, such as your hands, shoulders, eyebrows, and forehead. Also, and perhaps most important, stay away from hand gestures and pointing. At a minimum, it's distracting. Even more dangerous to your goal of being diplomatic, it can be perceived as aggressive.

> **Quick Quiz:** Think about the scenario from the beginning of this chapter. How would you apply the rules of diplomacy to that situation? Now that you're equipped with the tips for applying the rules, how would you handle the situation?

The good news is that diplomacy can be developed and cultivated in almost any situation. Of course, practice definitely helps. Fortunately, these principles can be applied not only in business but in our day-to-day personal interactions, both at home and with friends. In all of your relationships, try to make it a point to practice diplomacy. Your friendships and family life will be stronger for it in the end. With constant practice, diplomacy will come naturally to you in all of your business interactions, as well.

Summary: How to Speak with Tact and Grace

✓ Business diplomacy helps to achieve goals in a positive manner.
✓ There are consequences of not being diplomatic.
✓ Diplomatic communication is honest, yet polite and respectful.
✓ Three rules of diplomacy:
   1. Don't criticize.
   2. Be appreciative.
   3. See the other person's point of view.
✓ Diplomatic Process:
   1. Be observant and know the players.
   2. Observe communication style and flex.

3. Choose your words carefully.

4. Think, and be open.

5. Relax your body and face.

Smart Talk Challenge #1

Think about a recent, real-life conflict or situation with a coworker or business partner that you could have handled better. How could you have flexed your communication style to match theirs? Be as specific as possible. How might you have chosen your words differently?

Smart Talk Challenge #2

Talk about an emotional or challenging topic in the mirror; something that you're conflicted about. Observe your face closely. Are you showing anger? Are you showing any negative emotions? Now record yourself talking about the same difficult topic. Can you hear any negativity in your voice? Try both again, this time eliminating any behaviors that were outward signs of your negativity.

Smart Talk Challenge #3

Spend an entire day focusing on appreciation. Throughout the day, make a point to show and share sincere appreciation for others. Go the extra mile from an appreciation standpoint. Tell your family what it is that you appreciate about them. Tell each of your employees the traits you appreciate in them. Tell your boss what you appreciate about him or her. At the end of your appreciation day, tell yourself what you appreciate about yourself. I guarantee if you make a concerted effort at this, you will have a great day.

Case Study: Trisha Liu

XYZ e-mail marketing company creates effective e-mail campaigns on behalf of their customers and helps them to adhere to anti-spam regulations. XYZ needs to keep customers happy while at the same time policing their marketing actions. The team at XYZ has a particularly challenging job and asks for a single primary contact within each customer site to act as an internal audit liaison.

ABC Company hired XYZ. ABC identified Sue as their internal audit liaison. This meant that all of ABC's internal marketing staff was required to work with Sue on e-mail campaigns. However, month after month, frustration would arise between Sue and Joe, an ABC marketer who only occasionally ran e-mail campaigns. Joe didn't fully understand one of the crucial elements of the process that required him to limit his mailings. The rules and regulations that Sue constantly brought up didn't make sense to him.

From Sue's perspective, she was tired of explaining the same concepts month after month and was beginning to show outward signs of her frustration. She decided to call her contact, Trisha, at XYZ for some help. Sue knew that Trisha had reached out to Joe in the past and correctly recognized the value of the preexisting relationship.

Trisha was extremely well-trained in diplomatic communication. Trisha's goal was to have Joe feel able to get his job done while at the same time understand and accept the process that Sue had already explained several times. She understood that diplomatic communication is all in the delivery and it was important for both Sue and especially Joe to feel respected.

Trisha started by communicating to Joe that her goal was to achieve the best results possible for Joe. She wanted him to be successful. She broke down the concepts that Sue had been trying to get across into smaller chunks and kept checking in with Joe throughout their conversation to make sure she could provide any additional details as needed.

She also understood that it was important to avoid jargon and instead choose words that were simple and clear. She needed to be patient and meet Joe where he was. She needed her tone to remain soothing, reassuring and, most important, not condescending.

At the end of their conversation, Joe thanked Trisha for her patience and expertise.

I asked Trisha why she remembered this particular inter-action so many years later. She said, "That's when I realized that making the effort with diplomatic communication can really pay off."

Trisha Liu is an enterprise community manager at HP ArcSight.

6. Fearless Feedback:
How to Deliver Restorative Feedback

Feedback is the breakfast of champions.

—KEN BLANCHARD

LOU: Here's the report you asked for.

SUE: Finally!

LOU: I completed it as soon as I could.

SUE: You need to get the report in on time. Next time, it better be on time!

 Quick Quiz: Is this performance feedback or criticism? Think about a time when you received criticism. How did you feel? How did you react?

Criticism vs. Feedback

Winston Churchill said, "Criticism may not be agreeable, but it is necessary. It fulfills the same function as pain in the human body. It calls attention to an unhealthy state of things." I don't agree. Criticism isn't necessary. Criticism stinks. It's usually general, vague, focused on the person rather than on a behavior, and it's based on opinions or feelings. It's a negative judgment.

Like Lou, we've all been on the receiving end of angry criticism (aka, getting yelled at). And although delivering angry "feedback" may help you feel better, it's certainly not motivating for the person receiving the message. The goal of a change in behavior is unlikely to happen as a result of criticism.

Instead, for change to happen we need what I call *restorative feedback*. In medicine, restorative care is a planned, systematic process that focuses on helping patients to maintain the highest level of function. That's what managers should be doing in the workplace.

Why?

Because we all want and need feedback to help us improve, to get stronger, to be better. I want feedback from my customers (and from you, the readers) so that I know what to keep doing and what I can do better. My employees want feedback to know what is expected of them. My clients pay me for my feedback so they can learn and improve.

Feedback from others is one of the fastest ways to get better at something and it is crucial to improving productivity. All learning and growth happens through restorative feedback. Yet, most people don't get or give regular feedback. In fact, in April 2011 a Gallup study of 47,000 workers around the world showed respondents least often gave high ratings to items related to feedback. The report states, "This low ranking suggests that employers and managers don't provide workers with regular, individualized feedback."

 Quick Quiz: When was the last time you delivered any form of feedback or recognition? Have you delivered any feedback within the last week? Why or why not?

So What's with the Lack of Feedback?

Crickets heard from your patio during the last fleeting moments of summer sunlight are comforting and relaxing. On the other hand, crickets chirping down the halls of your office because the stressed-out boss is eerily silent, they elicit paranoia and hand wringing, even among the most confident and talented employees. People need feedback. Start talking.

I know from experience at many organizations that managers are often reluctant to give feedback. They resist. They'll say, "I don't have time for it," or "I'm not comfortable delivering feedback." They're concerned about damaging relationships or de-motivating productive team members. Sometimes, they're concerned that feedback won't create a change in behavior or won't generate the desired results.

Some managers assume they give enough feedback. Some managers assume they don't need to deliver feedback because either most employees will naturally know how they are doing or will assume they are doing fine. However, without effective feedback, without *restorative* feedback, organizations don't significantly improve productivity.

What Is Restorative Feedback?

Like restorative medicine or *restorative* justice, the word *restorative* emphasizes the need to return the relationship to a strong, healthy state. Restorative feedback is respectful, nonjudgmental, and collaborative. It requires active listening, facilitating dialogue, problem solving, and accountability.

Restorative feedback is what illuminates blind spots in a positive manner. ("Wow, I didn't know that! Thanks for telling me.") Restorative feedback is what reinforces and encourages a job well done. Restorative feedback is what builds confidence and self-esteem. Without restorative feedback employees don't grow and learn.

Feedback Motivates Changes in Behavior

Feedback is one of the most important management tools to motivate specific actions or reactions in a certain situation. Positive feedback encourages someone to keep doing certain behaviors. And restorative feedback motivates someone to act or react differently under given circumstances.

To be clear, restorative feedback is not asking someone to be a different person. Like a coach, a manager's role is to tell employees what they are doing right, to tell them how they can improve performance or show them how to do something new.

The Magic Ratio

Imagine if an athletic coach sat down with each player and delivered feedback *only once a year*. How useful would that be? Or imagine a coach who mostly provides negative feedback and rarely reinforces positive behaviors. Do you think the players would continue with the positive behaviors? How would that make a player feel? What if the coach had a wild celebration when a typically poor performer just met standards? How would that make the other players feel? It's likely that you intuitively understand what the research has confirmed.

If you want people to improve, you need to use a 5:1 positive to negative ratio. That's five "way to go's" to one "Oops." Interestingly, researchers found this ratio can predict, with remarkable accuracy, a number of things, including workplace performance[1] and divorce[2].

Psychologist John Gottman first studied positive-to-negative ratios in marriages. Using a 5:1 ratio, which Gottman called "The Magic Ratio," he and his colleagues predicted whether 700 newlywed couples would stay together or divorce by scoring their positive and negative interactions in one fifteen-minute conversation. Ten years later, the follow-up revealed that they had predicted divorce with 87 percent accuracy[3,4].

Commit to Persistent, Consistent Restorative Feedback

Leaders must set minimum standards of performance along with targets that will comfortably stretch and motivate people and follow up with feedback when targets are not reached or standards are breached. Leaders must persistently hold their team to the targets and standards, not just when things go wrong or at certain times of the year. In addition, leaders need to consistently apply the targets and standards. For example, if a typically high performer does not reach a target, the leader needs to manage the performance issue the same as he would for any other employee.

If you want your employees and teammates to grow, you need to make a commitment to persistent and consistent two-way feedback. You need to build a culture that values feedback. Reinforce that everyone deserves feedback and that providing feedback is a primary function of a manager or supervisor.

The best part is that persistent, consistent, restorative feedback creates a supportive environment built on trust. And the people around you will improve and become more satisfied because they are being coached to do better. Restorative feedback shows you care and that you're interested in helping the people around you. It shows that you are a wise leader.

Delivering regular feedback doesn't take more than a few minutes and it certainly doesn't have to be difficult or hurtful. In fact, by following Gottman's 5:1 ratio and the rules of restorative feedback, it can be quick, comfortable, and often welcomed.

When and Where Is Restorative Feedback Delivered?

Before I talk about technique, I want to answer two common questions about restorative feedback:

- *When* do you give praise or guidance?
- *Where* do you give praise or guidance?

The simple answer to the first question is that you should always give it as close to the behavior as possible so the event details are fresh in everyone's mind. The longer you wait, the more detached the feedback becomes from the behavior. It's best to address issues as they arise and reinforce positive behavior immediately so people know what to do more of.

In fact, if you do it quickly, matter-of-factly, directly, and *respectfully,* it is more likely to inspire a change in behavior. However, if you feel like you would be unable to deliver thoughtful and respectful feedback then it is best to wait until you are able to gather your thoughts and plan your words, even if that means waiting until the next day.

 Warning: The longer you wait, the more likely the person will feel like they are in trouble or unappreciated.

Try to catch and respond to employees doing the job right more often than you catch and respond to them doing something not quite right—and, please, please, please, don't just acknowledge how they are performing only once or twice a year at review time!

To answer the second question, I think feedback often gets postponed because we believe that it should always be delivered behind closed doors. However, positive and restorative feedback (for information or awareness) can be delivered directly and quickly as long as the feedback is delivered somewhat privately to the receiver. This means you could take the employee aside and quietly clue them in. It could be directly after a meeting, after everyone else has left the room. Or perhaps restorative feedback could be delivered in the car when returning from a client appointment or on the way to a group lunch. Deliver out of earshot of others, but not necessarily behind closed doors.

Finally, let your direct reports know that a normal part of their development is to receive regular feedback from you. This way, they won't be surprised or feel blindsided when you pull them aside and offer them a few thoughtful words.

Many young leaders struggle with learning and practicing feedback techniques. Delivering effective feedback is not a natural gift or aptitude. However, it is a skill that can be learned with adequate practice and proper coaching. (It's a skill I teach through role-play and most participants pick it up quickly.) Good technique plus persistent and consistent feedback is what makes for a strong communicator.

Smart Talk Technique for Giving Restorative Feedback

Do not follow the feedback "sandwich approach" that involves delivering praise, then offering constructive criticism, and closing with more praise. Although the sandwich approach is commonly recommended, it is not effective communication. It's like a fake pat on the back, followed by a sucker punch, followed by another fake pat on the back. It certainly doesn't benefit the receiver because it waters down the feedback so that the key message isn't as clear. Here are the steps for delivering effective restorative feedback:

Step #1: Identify the Desired Outcome

Before you do anything, ask yourself: What is the goal of your feedback? Is it to provide information or awareness? "I noticed that when Suzanne is part of our meetings, you tend to interact less. Why do you think that is?" Or are you communicating a major setback, a final warning before firing, or serious allegation? "Last night the door was left unlocked and we were robbed. You were the last one to leave." Identifying your outcome will help you plan your words.

Step #2: Ask for Permission (or Prepare for Feedback)

If your feedback is primarily informative or for growth purposes, you'll want to first be sure the person is interested in receiving your feedback. This requires that you've laid the groundwork for a trusting relationship and that you ask for permission. Especially if he or she hasn't specifically requested your feedback, it's always good to ask. "Would you be interested in some feedback on the meeting and how I see your contributions to our process? Could we get together sometime?" "Would you like for me to share something with you that I noticed?" If the feedback is delicate or perhaps hard to hear, it helps to prepare the person by sharing your intention. "I have tremendous respect for you and your work. But I'd like to share something with you that I hope will help you be even better."

Quick Quiz: Think about the last time you delivered feedback. Did you ask permission to provide the feedback? The last time you received feedback did they ask you first? How did you feel?

Step #3: Focus on Controllable and Repeated Behaviors

Focus your feedback on behaviors that the employee has control over. Remember, the goal of feedback is to change future relevant behavior. So there is no point in giving feedback on something the employee can't change or is likely to never happen again; it will only serve to damage trust.

Step #4: Be Respectfully Direct

Be direct when delivering your message. Get to the point and avoid beating around the bush.

 Warning: Don't sugarcoat bad news. Most people will appreciate your honesty and that builds trust.

Both negative and positive feedback should be given in a straightforward, but sincere manner. Sincerity says that you mean what you say with care and respect.

For example, here's the typical feedback Lou might receive from his supervisor:

> Lou, I know you've been working hard on this project, but I'm tired of waiting for you to get me your weekly report. Stop being lazy. You need to start getting your reports in on time! And you expect to get a raise at review time?

None of this is helpful or useful to Lou. First, there is a mixed message created by the initial "but." Most of us are aware that once a "but" (or a "however" or and "although") is uttered, you've signaled to the other person not to believe the first part of the sentence. Even if the first part of the sentence is in fact true, that "but" just muddles the main message. It's better to be direct.

Instead of telling Lou what he shouldn't be (lazy); his manager needs to tell him specifically what he should do differently.

Next, the "need to" phrase isn't useful. Again, telling Lou he needs to . . . doesn't give him enough information to correct the behavior. And, of course, the last line is just mean-spirited.

Step #5: Describe the Specific Behaviors

Describe behavioral acts instead of attitudes or personality. Start your statements with an "I" message, such as, "I noticed," "I observed," "I saw."

For example, "I noticed that for the past two weeks the report has been late by one day." Or "I noticed that you don't include a signature line with your contact information on your e-mails." Or "I notice that at times you lead our discussions off on tangents. For example . . ."

At this point, your goal is to simply reflect back the behavior as if you were a mirror. This should just be a brief review of your observations so that the person understands what behaviors you're talking about.

 Warning: Don't rely on secondhand stories, particularly for sensitive feedback. Use your own, direct experiences.

If the goal of your conversation is awareness, then after you deliver your observations you should pause. In fact, I recommend pausing for a full 3–5 seconds. This subtly encourages and allows the individual to respond.

If there is no response, then invite the person to offer his or her view by asking "What happened?" in a neutral tone. This provides an opportunity to reflect on the event and why the behavior may have occurred. In academic medicine, this type of informal awareness intervention is referred to as a "cup of coffee conversation,[5]" which is a very appropriate way to describe it.

This gives the person the opportunity to give self-feedback and to evaluate and identify areas for improvement, instead of the leader offering his observations. It then makes it more natural for the leader to agree and/or express his or her specific recommendations for professional behavior.

Step #6: State the Impact of the Behavior

However, in some situations, before offering specific recommendations, sometimes it helps to clearly state the impact or consequence of the observed behavior. "When your report is late, it holds up my report; or worse, it sometimes forces me to turn in my report without your contribution. We value your thoughtful comments and without them the departmental report isn't complete and it becomes more difficult for Dave to make good decisions." Or "When you don't include your contact information, it makes it difficult for clients to find your phone number quickly." Be as detailed, specific, and concrete as possible. Clearly state your performance expectations. Observations are far more factual and nonjudgmental than when you state your opinion or analysis of what you saw.

Step #7: Express Appreciation or Concern

If your feedback is positive, you also need to express appreciation. Keep in mind that appreciation without the specific feedback is just vague praise. And when praise is added to positive feedback, it becomes much more powerful.

"Lou, I know how difficult it is to turn this report around so quickly. Thanks for getting it on time this week. I really appreciate your efforts and your thoughtful remarks that you included this week."

If the feedback is restorative, then express your concern. Again, a good communicator always communicates with sincerity. And a tone of concern will communicate that you care and that the feedback is important. Your goal is to be perceived as a problem solver, not as an attacker.

"Lou, I'm wondering if there is something I can do to make sure you have enough time to complete the report by the deadline. It seems Monday is your busiest day. Would it make it easier for you to have the report due on Friday instead of Monday?"

At times, no matter how effectively you've delivered your observations, the person receiving the feedback may attempt to blame the behavior on others. In this case, it's important to remind the person that he or she is required to respond in a professional manner no matter what mistakes were made by others. If possible, also point out that it's the specific behavior or specific disruptive event that is at issue, and that you value his or her other contributions to the organization.

Step #8: Define Next Steps

The final step is tricky. You might decide to just leave it there and let the person decide what to do on their own. If you pause long enough just after describing the impact, people will often volunteer a plan of restorative action on their own. If not, you may want to ask if they have any ideas to correct or improve the situation.

"Lou, I'm wondering if you might have any suggestions that might help you to complete the report by the deadline?"

As a manager, you may need to describe and ask for specific changes. A concrete plan needs to be in place so as to encourage action. For example, the plan can be subtle: "Would you consider adding a signature line?" Or "Would you prefer to turn the report in on Friday?" Or more direct: "Please add a signature line to your e-mails and send it to me by the end of the day."

Step #9: Keep Documentation

At a minimum, supervisors should keep notes on any performance problems discussed with the employee, including the date, the issues and the performance expectations communicated to the employee. However, depending on the situation, a more formal performance follow-up plan could also be created and shared with the employee. Encourage employees to also keep record of feedback given and received, also noting what was learned from each experience.

So here's how it might sound all together:

"Hey, would you like some feedback? I noticed that you don't include a signature line in your e-mails. When there's no signature line it makes it difficult for clients to find your telephone number quickly. It can be especially frustrating when they are in a hurry. Would you consider adding a signature line?"

Here's the example for Lou:

"Would you like me to share something I've noticed?"

[yes]

"For the past two weeks, the report has been late by one day. When your report is late, it holds up my report. Worse, it sometimes forces me to turn in my report without your contribution. We value your thoughtful comments and without them the departmental report isn't complete and it becomes more difficult for Dave to make good decisions.

"I'm wondering if there is something I can do to make sure you have enough time to complete the report by the deadline. It seems Monday is your busiest day. Would it make it easier for you to have the report due on Friday instead of Monday? Or maybe you've got a better suggestion that will help you to complete the report by the deadline?"

Ultimately, the person should walk away clear about exactly what was done and what he or she needs to do differently next time. If you sincerely focus on the fact that your goal with feedback is to motivate a change in behavior, it should no longer feel uncomfortable. And if you provide feedback regularly, then it doesn't need to take more than a few minutes.

By now you might be thinking, "Constructive criticism—oops,

I mean *restorative feedback*—is complicated. It sounds risky, and it will take extra effort on my part." Yes, all of that is true. However, it's important to recognize that many times employees or colleagues are unaware of their own behavior or the consequences of their behavior. It's the role of a leader to guide employees with early interventions and prohibit patterns of unwanted behavior to become routine.

If you value the people around you and you value yourself, you will find following this process worth the risks and worth the possibility of a few losses while developing your technique. Because in the end, effectively and successfully delivering restorative feedback will provide you and those around you with significant gains in productivity and satisfaction.

 Check This Out: See what *not* to do when it comes to delivering feedback! www.smarttalksuccess.com/extras the 2008 Slamdance Film Festival short entry *Feedback*.

Summary: How to Deliver Restorative Feedback

✓ Criticism is general, vague, and focused on the person (not on the behavior).

✓ Mangers are often reluctant to deliver feedback, although it is the best way to improve productivity.

✓ Restorative feedback in the workplace is a systematic process that focuses on helping employees maintain the highest level of productivity.

✓ Restorative feedback is respectful, nonjudgmental, and collaborative and requires active listening, facilitating dialogue, problem solving, and accountability.

✓ To have more success with restorative feedback, use a 5:1 positive feedback to negative feedback ratio.

✓ Restorative feedback creates a supportive environment built on trust.

✓ Deliver feedback one-on-one as close to the behavior as possible while details are fresh.

✓ Deliver feedback out of earshot of others, not necessarily behind closed doors.

✓ The restorative feedback process:
1. Identify your desired outcome.
2. Ask for permission or prepare for feedback.
3. Focus on controllable or repeated behaviors.
4. Be respectfully direct.
5. Describe specific behaviors.
6. State the impact of the behaviors.
7. Express concern (or appreciation).
8. Define next steps.
9. Keep documentation.

Smart Talk Challenge #1
The next time you are about to deliver feedback, think about two different ways you could first ask for permission to give the feedback.

Smart Talk Challenge #2
Think about something that a colleague or employee does that really bothers you. Can you describe these activities or behaviors objectively and respectfully?

Smart Talk Challenge #3
Based on the scenario from challenge #2 create a restorative dialog that might be used to change that person's behavior. Write it out. Then record yourself delivering the feedback, without your notes. Review the video to see how you do. How would you feel if someone delivered your feedback to you?

Case Study: Andrall Pearson

Andrall Pearson was president of PepsiCo from 1971 to 1984. He was featured on the cover of *Fortune Magazine* as one of the "10 toughest bosses" in 1980. According to writer Andrew Parker, "Pearson was dismissive of his employees work, drove them hard to achieve results and otherwise motivated through fear." During his presidency, annual revenue grew to nearly $8 billion from $1.1 billion.

However, at seventy-two he was asked to come out of retirement to help PepsiCo transition some of its acquisitions (Taco Bell, Pizza Hut, KFC) into what was eventually called Yum Brands. He became chairman of a spinoff, and joining Mr. Pearson was David Novak, the heir-apparent and president.

Novak was described as a kinetic and charismatic leader. He took an active interest in people to help them achieve their potential. In fact, in a 2009 *New York Times* interview Mr. Novak said:

"What I think a great leader does, a great coach does, is understand what kind of talent you have and then you help people leverage that talent so that people can achieve what they never thought they were capable of. The only way you can do that is to care about the people who work for you. No one's going to care about you unless you care about them. But if you care about someone, genuinely, then they're going to care about you because you're making a commitment and an investment in them.

"You show you care by really taking an active interest in the people working for you, and you care enough to give them direct feedback. People are starved for direct feedback. People want to hear how they can do better. Too many leaders don't provide that feedback. So if you take an active interest in someone, you take an active interest in sharing with them your perspective on what they can do to improve."[6]

The interesting part of the story is that Mr. Pearson admired Mr. Novak so much that he decided to emulate Novak's leadership style. According to Andrew Parker, "What happened was a remarkable transformation that is still talked about to this day. Pearson went from being the gruff, demanding boss, to one that provided quality feedback and listened intently from his direct reports in order to get the most out of them."

It's incredible to me that a man as successful as Mr. Pearson, at age seventy-two, was willing and able to change into a wise and effective communicator.

7. Ouch, That Hurts!
How to Accept Criticism

All good criticism should be judged the way art is. You shouldn't read it the way you read history or science.

—Leslie Fiedler

You just finished a project. You put a ton of effort into it and you are proud of your work. The next day your boss sends you an e-mail saying he thought this wasn't your best. He tells you that when he reviewed it he noticed a number of errors and that overall the work was sloppy.

 Quick Quiz: How would that e-mail make you feel? What would you do? How would you handle this scenario?

No one likes the sting of criticism, especially if it was delivered harshly or came unexpectedly. But whether we like it or not, criticism is inevitable. Especially as we build large social networks, make public presentations, or act in positions of leadership. The more people we know, the more may like us—but also the more that may criticize.

Handle Criticism by Practicing a Response

Sometimes you'll be caught off guard by a criticism, so an initial reaction of anger and the desire to defend ourselves, or worse, to lash out is perfectly normal. However, by practicing some healthy responses, you'll have a much better chance of keeping a damaging reaction at bay.

 Warning: Don't react immediately. Good communicators don't get defensive or emotional.

You have to know ahead of time what works the best for you in times of stress. Perhaps you'll want to turn your face away, take a deep breath, or count to eleven. Just do whatever it takes to pause a moment.

If the person delivering the criticism isn't directly in front of you (as in a critical e-mail, for example), you don't have to react right away anyway. If possible, step away from the criticism. Go for a walk, do yoga, or talk with a friend to help calm you down. Let the critical e-mail sit in your inbox a full day before you reply.

Practice a planned criticism response enough so that you can calmly, consistently, and automatically react to criticism, whenever or wherever you receive it. Perhaps say, "Thanks for taking time to share that with me. I sincerely appreciate the feedback." The last thing you want is to get angry at the other person (and yourself) for poorly handling the situation.

The easiest way to accept criticism is to understand that everyone makes mistakes and there is always room for improvement. I like to also keep in mind that it's normal for others to have opinions different from mine. Although it may be hard to accept in the moment, criticism is actually a gift in disguise because it can help you grow by illuminating blind spots. Finally, particularly at work, the intention of criticism is usually to help you improve your performance (it's not typically intended to be mean-spirited). It's meant to help you do better work, even though it may be poorly delivered. (See chapter 6 for more on how to deliver helpful feedback).

Always evaluate the perspectives of others with an open mind. I'm not suggesting you automatically accept another person's point of view, but instead to give it due consideration, no matter how negative the delivery. I know, easier said than done.

Buy Some Time with Silence

Though you can't control the other person, you can influence him or her with your response. If the person delivering the criticism is right in front of you, your choice to remain silent, turn away for a bit, or take a breath buys you time and may be a gift to them as well. A silent, nonreactive, neutral stare jams and sometimes deflects the shower of negative energy and often bewilders the other person. Don't worry if the person asks, "Why aren't you responding?" You can just say in earnest, "I'm listening."

Since we rarely know all the circumstances of someone's life, give them space to re-listen to their words. Remember that your criticizer is a real person. They may have just had a fight with someone, are having financial trouble, or are dealing with a sudden onset of middle-aged acne. Some people just aren't very sensitive to the feelings of others, but I choose to believe that most people are not mean-spirited. Give them a minute to possibly take back their words—or at least acknowledge how they said them.

Another reason to avoid an immediate, defensive reaction is that in most cases, you'll only be adding to the problem. As I see it, reacting tends to come from emotion and often just adds more fuel to an already volatile situation. A cooling off time allows you to move beyond an initial negative emotional reaction and respond with thoughtful consideration.

We particularly feel the need to defend ourselves if a criticism is delivered in public. We have the urge to attack the attacker. But if you can rise above the attack and remain positive in the face of an assault, others will notice and admire you. (I've had many people write to me complimenting me on how I've handled public criticism.) Perhaps more important, you'll feel good because you didn't stoop to the level of empty criticism and attack.

 Quick Quiz: Can you recall a time when you received harsh public criticism? How did you deal with it? Did you receive praise for your ability to handle the situation effectively? Why or why not?

Diffuse Criticism with Gratitude

A short, simple way to quickly diffuse criticism is to say, "Thank you." Often gratitude for criticism is unexpected and, surprisingly, appreciated. It helps to remind me that behind every criticism is an opportunity for growth. It reminds me not to take criticism as a personal attack or insult. I prefer to view it as reflection on a behavior that I now have the opportunity to review with fresh eyes.

The next step is to paraphrase the criticism as restorative feedback. However, if you sense that you are in control of your emotions, you might also explore the criticism with curiosity. "Thanks for letting me know. Can you tell me more so I can understand better?"

Don't assume you understand the other person's perceptions or intentions. It's best to directly ask if they don't automatically offer. You could also say, "Can you help me understand why you think that?" "Can you give me specific examples?" "What was your impression when . . . ?" It helps to not be certain about your own perspective. Your curiosity and openness allow the other person to perceive that you are approachable and want to have a discussion about the issue. However, if you feel blindsided and not yet ready for more details, you can choose to skip that.

Of course, don't resort to name-calling or blame. Up to this point, your only goal is to try to understand the criticism. Use this as an opportunity to get helpful observations and details. After you have a good understanding of the other person's point of view you can paraphrase what your heard. If you are open to learning, these questions can help you better understand and modify your behavior.

Sometimes you'll receive criticism from a source that is unknown or anonymous. In this case, you'll need to try to transform the criticism into restorative feedback (see chapter 6). For example, suppose you are reading an evaluation form from a presentation you just delivered and an anonymous reviewer wrote, "Your presentation was boring." Your could think, "What a jerk, what does he know! He didn't even put his name on the form." Instead you could think, "Hmm, maybe I should consider adding more forms of audience engagement to my presentation. I'll ask Sue what she thought and see if she has any suggestions."

 Quick Quiz: Think of criticism you received most recently. How might you transform it into restorative feedback?

An Example of How to Deal with Criticism

I remember when a listener to my Public Speaker podcast gave me feedback about what she perceived as a "forced chuckle." Initially I responded by saying, "Thanks for the feedback." (Well, I must admit that was after my initial thought of, "I don't have a forced chuckle!")

Later I decided to explore this perspective (with curiosity) by asking others on The Public Speaker Facebook page whether anyone else held a similar opinion. One person responded that they agreed with the comment, so I decided to ask her to help me understand her perspective better. To be clear, I wasn't necessarily agreeing with the perception. However, I did appreciate the information and I was (and am) open to learn more. It's unrealistic to assume that you, your style, and your ideas are always going to be well received by everyone, so it is best to be prepared for the times that it will not strike the right chord.

Vent Appropriately

After you've practiced a response and bought some time, you may still feel angry, frustrated, or upset. Don't get swept up into the negative vortex. Find a healthy way to release those emotions that came from the critical conversation.

If the source of the criticism is someone with whom you have an important relationship, don't hurt the relationship by saying something regrettable. Be angry and upset privately. I often write an e-mail in which I allow myself to say whatever I want (no filters), even things that I know aren't true. The sole objective is to express my angry feelings. Of course, I never actually send the e-mail. (In fact, I always make sure to put my own name in the "To" field because I never want to accidentally send this e-mail to anyone.)

Writing this note allows me to organize my thoughts and clarify my feelings. After I have had time to cool off I usually delete the message—and then I'm ready to face the situation more objectively. (Occasionally I'll keep a note like this just to remind myself of my blurred perspective when I'm angry and hurt.) The main point is that you need to plan your conversation and not have an off-the-cuff emotionally heated discussion.

 Quick Quiz: What is your preferred method of expressing your anger? Do you protect your important relationships?

A Word of Caution About Venting

That's what friends are (not necessarily) for. Many people like to vent to supportive friends and coworkers. That can be healthy, within reason. However, if the friends might be negatively influenced by learning of the situation (for example, they work for the same person who criticized you), you may want to pick someone else—someone more objective.

Remember that our negativity toward a person can rub off on friends or fellow coworkers who may not have had any preexisting problem with that individual. It's not professional to foster a nega-tive culture and defeating teamwork just so you can feel better.

Give Thought to the Feedback

The next step may be hardest. You need to listen and reflect. But in order to really listen, you need to first shut up and be quiet. You need to turn off your defenses. You need to quiet down the voice in your head that wants to respond impulsively. Probably most important for me, I need to remember to keep my face and body neutral—no eye rolling or sighs.

After getting away from the situation, give some thought to the actual statement the person made and honestly ask yourself, "Is there a grain of truth in this?" or "What can I learn from this?" One way to determine if the criticism is valid is to reflect on the strength of your initial emotional response.

If you felt deeply about the criticism, it may be because it struck a nerve and concerns something that is very important to you. If it only irritated (or amused) you, it may have fallen lower on your value scale. For example, if someone criticized how you handled a particular work situation, you may feel stronger emotions than if they suggested that, "Yellow is not your best color." (Unless of course, your style is very important to you!)

Keep in mind that there's a fine line between thinking about a situation and obsessing over it. To check that, consider your mo-tives for hanging onto the thought. Are you obsessing so you can grow and learn, or is it because your ego just can't accept the criti-cism?

Separate the Emotion from the Person

Next, it's important to separate the content of the feedback from any negative emotions, or the way the feedback was presented. Ask yourself, "If this same suggestion had been delivered gently from a caring friend, would I give it more credence?"

Also think about frequency. Have you heard this feedback from more than one source on more than one occasion? Are people you love and trust mentioning it to you? Is there a pattern developing? If so, it may be time to give the feedback some serious consideration.

A friend told me about a time when three different people in her life separately reminded her of a certain negative tendency. The combined feedback helped her understand her behavior and make a positive change. It may help to discuss the criticism with a trusted advisor, who can give you a more objective view and possibly offer some suggestions for handling the situation effectively.

Decide How to Respond

If, after reasonable thought, you decide that the criticism was not justified, or not particularly important, you can either ignore the comment and move on (nothing says you have to respond to every e-mail, for example) or leave it at the simple "Thank you for your comment."

Or perhaps you found the feedback to only be partly true. Be careful not to ignore the part that you do find to be true. You'll still need to create a plan to solve that part of the problem.

If ultimately you thought the feedback (either in part or in totality) was valid and helpful (no matter how it was delivered), contact the person (by e-mail, note, or in person) and genuinely thank them for taking the time to point out the issue. You may even briefly explain what steps you are taking to improve in that area. Who knows? You may begin to develop a relationship with them!

Move On

The final step is to move on. This is easier said than done. At this point, you need to either 1) ignore the comment or make only a cursory response, or 2) incorporate the feedback into your personal growth plan.

If you are choosing to ignore the criticism, then stop your thoughts from revisiting it. Replace them with your decision to move on (i.e., remind yourself "That is done. Over. Fini. Kaput.").

If, however, you've decided to make a change, then develop a plan. Do you need to write things down more? Do you need to make extra effort to greet people during meetings? Do you need to practice proper pronunciation of a particular word? Do what you have to do to train yourself to benefit from the suggestion, create a plan, and follow up.

Ultimately, it's important not to hold a grudge. Put the mistake out of your mind and focus on how you will best be able to move forward. If possible, clear the air by letting the person know how you would prefer to receive corrective or restorative feedback in the future (maybe buy them a copy of this book and leave it on their seat with a bookmark in chapter 6). Ultimately, it's important to recognize that people who provide you criticism help you to grow. Remember it's not *you* that is being criticized, it's a behavior that you can change if you choose to.

Summary: How to Accept Criticism

✓ The easiest way to accept criticism is to understand that everyone makes mistakes and there is always room for improvement.

✓ Welcome the perspective of others with an open mind.

✓ Don't emotionally react to criticism. Instead, respond with thoughtful consideration.

✓ Diffuse criticism with gratitude, it will be unexpected and appreciated.

✓ Always convert criticism into restorative feedback.

✓ Process for handling criticism:
   1. Listen and objectively review and explore the criticism with curiosity.
   2. Vent appropriately any feelings of anger or frustration.
   3. View criticism as restorative feedback and reflect on how things might be different if you changed your behavior.
   4. Separate the content of the feedback from the person who delivered it and the way it was delivered.

5. Decide how to respond.
6. Choose to take corrective steps, or not.
7. Move on.

Smart Talk Challenge #1
Convert the following criticism into restorative feedback. "The information you gave me this morning was all screwed up. I felt like an idiot at the meeting when I didn't have the proper information."

Smart Talk Challenge #2
Have a friend criticize you. Choose three things you are particularly sensitive about and create the exact words you want them to say to you. Have them repeat your words in a mean tone for five minutes straight. The idea is for you to become desensitized to feedback and practice a neutral silent response.

Smart Talk Challenge #3
Think about a time where you attacked someone with criticism. What were the underlying reasons for your behavior? Did your harsh words stem entirely from the actions and behaviors of other person? Use this exercise to help you understand why someone might react in a particular way that has little or nothing to do with you.

Case Study: Kathleen Walker

"Many years ago, I aspired to be a published author and applied for a women-only author grant from a private foundation. The woman responsible for reading the grant requests sent a scathing letter back to me that I needed to be more professional, take some creative writing classes, and perfect my manuscript before I even considered going forward.

"I cried when I read her letter.

"I thought her to be Victorian in her attitude, and even initially discounted her hurtful words. I was stung by her blunt comments. However over time and in doing my own research on how to be a published author, I painfully found that she was correct!

"I very much needed to learn more, be more professional, and perfect my work before going forward. I did as she suggested and took some creative writing courses at the local college. I studied published authors and their bios to see how to follow in their footsteps. I learned a lot from that very proper woman's blunt words and although they were very painful at the time, they were just the catalyst I needed.

"I'm happy to say I've had poetry and short stories published all over the world in prestigious publications and have published two books. I am grateful for the constructive criticism given way back when I needed it, even though I didn't know I needed it at the time. I subsequently sent a letter to her acknowledging how helpful her words to me were and thanked her for being honest with me."

8. We Have to Talk:
How to Have a Difficult Conversation

You're trying so hard to understand their mind, just speaking the truth without being unkind.

—"Difficult Conversation," by Neil Swanson
and Geoff Judges

You have to tell one of your most productive employees that she dresses inappropriately and unprofessionally. Worse, her personal hygiene is sometimes less than desirable. How do you handle this difficult conversation?

There's no way your team is going to meet the deadline and the project is likely to go over budget. As project manager, how will you share this information with the senior team and the client?

The newest sales engineer worked on the software demonstration all night. During the presentation, the software kept crashing and the presentation was a disaster. You have to talk to the sales engineer and her manager to make sure this doesn't happen again.

You are a consultant and have exceeded your client's budget. You need to ask for additional fees for the work you completed.

Quick Quiz: Think about a difficult conversation that you've had. How did it make you feel? How did you react?

It's widely accepted that if someone has spinach in their teeth, you will move heaven and earth to try and discreetly let them know. Why, then, is it so hard to tell that same person that their twenty-pounds-too-small and twenty-years-too-young shirt is wildly inappropriate for the office?

Difficult conversations cause most of us some level of anxiety. Discussing sensitive topics or delivering bad news is something most leaders dread. Often leaders have to fight the natural impulse to avoid confronting difficult issues. We're taught "Don't open that can of worms" and we may tell ourselves, "I'm too busy to deal with it right now, and besides, dealing with it will likely bruise our relationship—and it probably won't change anything anyway."

 Quick Quiz: Have you ever avoided difficult conversations? What was the consequence of avoiding? How much money and productivity is lost by not directly addressing inefficient employees or disgruntled workers?

Why We Shouldn't Avoid Difficult Conversations

Confronting another person is difficult. Perhaps it's because these skills are rarely taught at home or school. And even people with excellent communication skills sometimes retreat when faced with stressful or sensitive communication issues. No one wants or likes an awkward work environment and it seems easier (in the short term) to avoid things we don't like.

Warning: Avoiding conflict and difficult discussions is likely to do more damage than directly addressing the issue. Failure to have difficult conversations disrupts productivity and can directly impact profits.

When you avoid communication, the vacuum gets filled with negative assumptions and ill will. Relationships flounder. Very small matters can bloom into conflicts that become "unmentionable." In fact, a 2007 survey (sponsored by Nationwide) reported that because of failure to discuss a difficult issue, nearly half of the respondents lost sleep, 10 percent reported poor health, and 5 percent reported a loss of a job or friendship.

Worse, these "elephant in the room" conflicts sometimes grow so *huge* that eventually they blow up and demand your attention whether you're ready or not. So it's best to plan for and address difficult conversations before emotions run high. Having regular status meetings to discuss progress and possible issues is the best way to avoid difficult conversations altogether. The longer issues remain unaddressed the bigger the negative impact to your organization's performance.

Nobody wants to deliver bad news, especially to good people. Keep in mind that difficult conversations are difficult for everyone, not just you. How you handle these conversations will limit or enable success; for you and the other person. By addressing difficult issues, employees will know where they stand and what they need to change. In fact, if handled well, it's possible to make the person more engaged and feel good about it.

In chapter 6, I outlined the eight steps for delivering restorative feedback. Although difficult conversations certainly count as feedback, often sensitive or stressful issues require some extra steps to ensure effective communication. Those additional steps are covered in this chapter.

If you want to maintain your relationship with the other party, the goal is to encourage a change in behavior, and that means you need to deliver bad news thoughtfully, tactfully, and respectfully. So how do you do that? Here are the steps to achieving a positive outcome from a difficult conversation.

Step #1: Consider the Other Person's Perspective

When preparing for a difficult conversation it's critically important to think about the emotional and intellectual perspective of the other person. If you were that person, what would you be feeling and thinking? What would be important to you? How would you want to be treated?

Compassion helps you to be open to the other person's perspective. Compassion is what reminds us that other person is just doing the best they can with what they've got.

A common example is when you need to communicate that an important deadline will be missed or that project cost overruns have occurred. By stepping into the shoes of management and/or your clients, you can best prepare for the conversation. Plans have been developed based on the original commitments, so if a change to those plans is expected, then it is critical that management and/or the clients are notified as soon as possible so that alternative plans can be put in place. At the same time, management needs to recognize that you have done your best to meet the agreed upon deadlines and budgets.

For particularly sensitive issues, it may even be helpful to gain an understanding of how you and the other person typically manage conflict. In fact, in my team-building seminars, I have found it helpful to have participants complete a conflict assessment to first understand their style of conflict management. A very well-known model for understanding how people respond to conflict was developed by two psychologists, Thomas and Kilmann, in the early 1970s and has been in use for more than thirty-five years. The Thomas-Kilmann Conflict Mode Instrument[1] identifies five basic ways of dealing with conflict.

- Competitive: I win, you lose. This type of individual is assertive and uncooperative. He will pursue his own concerns at the expense of the relationship.
- Accommodator: You win, I lose. This type of individual is unassertive and cooperative, the complete opposite of the competitive style. For this person the relationship is more important than the conflict or winning.
- Avoider: I lose, you lose. This person is unassertive and uncooperative. He doesn't deal with conflict. He avoids, withdraws, or postpones.
- Collaborator: I win, you win. This type of individual is both assertive and cooperative; the complete opposite of the avoider.
- Compromiser: My way, your way. This type of individual is moderate in both assertiveness and cooperativeness. Compromisers give up more than accommodators but less than avoiders.

 Quick Quiz: What is your preferred style of conflict management? Does it change depending on who you are in conflict with or what the conflict is about? Think about your boss. What do you think is his or her preferred style of dealing with conflict?

Step #2: Prepare for a Difficult Conversation

None of us have a single style of dealing with conflict, but we do tend to rely on a specific style more heavily than on others. To manage a difficult conversation successfully, it's important to understand your own conflict management style as well as that of your conversation partner. You'll also want to consider the magnitude of the issue. For example, is this a major setback, a final warning before firing, a termination, or a serious allegation on the level of harassment? You'll need to think about and plan for reactions that might be difficult for you to handle.

It will be important to get your emotions under control as

well. Particularly for sensitive topics, you may initially react by making immediate judgments and casting blame. It's important to change your orientation instead to genuine curiosity so that you can be open to learning.

The best approach is to assume that you might have overlooked something. Ask yourself, "If I did contribute to this problem, in what ways could that be?" It's important to recognize that your behaviors could possibly be part of the problem.

Sometimes that's not enough. If it's a really important relationship and you don't want to hurt it (by saying something stupid), you'll need to gain an even broader perspective. If possible, talk to a mutually trusted third party to help you understand the situation even better and clearly identify what went wrong. Often a third party can present a point of view or advice without emotional attachment. A trusted advisor can often provide more clarity on the situation and enable you to understand better how the other person might view the situation.

If you don't have someone to go to for support, instead try to find others who have already gone through the same issue. Or you might want to try to find an expert who has dealt with the same issue many times before; they can help you understand the possible best approaches and possible alternative responses. Ultimately the responsibility of a good communicator is to anticipate concerns and questions and have all the information researched and ready.

 Quick Quiz: Who in your professional network is able to provide insight and perspective on particularly difficult issues that you might face? What steps have you taken to cultivate that relationship?

Think about where, when, and who needs to be part of each difficult conversation. Respect and privacy are important. You want to talk in a location where you won't be distracted or disturbed. If it's a serious or highly sensitive issue, then having another person in the room is sometimes necessary. But keep in mind that can be very intimidating and even counterproductive.

Let's look at Jane's case. Jane is a podcast listener and she reached out to me with a problem. It seems that she interrupted the phone call of the new employee in her group in order to give him some restorative feedback. The employee then went to their mutual boss and made a complaint about Jane, claiming that she was eavesdropping on his calls. The manager decided to directly address the issue with Jane and called a meeting that included a representative from HR. Jane was in shock. Since Jane had recently been promoted and was the senior person on the team, she thought that her behavior was supportive and helpful, rather than intrusive. After the meeting, Jane decided not to interact with the new employee at all and instead listen to an iPod throughout the day. Of course, this made everyone uncomfortable.

Step #3: Address Possible Issues Ahead of Time

For missed deadlines and serious issues, a root-cause analysis of why the issue occurred needs to be performed. In addition, the risk of more issues (as a result of the same problem) also needs to be analyzed. By identifying factors that contributed to the issue, you can possibly work around them or prevent them going forward. Plan and practice your message with another person so that you are sure you are being direct and clear.

I suggested that Jane talk directly with the new employee. Jane was hesitant. I suggested she take him to lunch (neutral territory) to discuss what had happened, or at a minimum to clarify roles and responsibilities since that seemed to be the root of the issue. This clarification would help prevent the issue from coming up again. We discussed possible reactions and responses, the different ways to approach the conversation, and the consequences of leaving the situation as it is.

Jane waited a few days so she could calmly discuss what had happened with the new employee. That's a good idea. We often need time to marinate and digest difficult issues. Be sure to allow plenty of time for yourself and the other party.

Jane had initially planned to explain why she had interrupted the phone call and to possibly discuss the overlap in their roles. With difficult conversations, if you start early enough, you can move slowly. The goal of the initial conversation is to be informative. That makes it easier for the other person to take the news—nothing has to change just yet. The hope is that the person will, in time, make a decision, improve, or take action on his or her own terms. However, eventually the conversations may need to move toward a goal of persuasion.

Step #4: State Your Observations

When you bring up the issue with the other person, it's best to start by describing the problematic behavior. Give bad news up front. Tough messages should be simple, specific, and clearly stated. If you're not specific, the person will likely think the feedback is about them as a person and not about their work.

For example, "I felt your comments in the meeting were inappropriate," or "The project will be one week late and the expected increase cost will be five thousand dollars." In addition, don't talk about motives. Say "The software crashed four times during the demonstration," not "The software crashed four times during the demonstration because you're lazy and you didn't do a run-through ahead of time." We often mistake people's underlying motives, and it just angers the person when they are misunderstood.

However, also keep in mind that although difficult conversations involve facts, the bottom line is that difficult conversations are often about conflicting perceptions, values, and feelings. It's not about what the contract says, it's about what the contract means. It's not about what is true, it's about what's perceived. Often difficult conversations can't be boiled down to "right" and "wrong" and that's exactly what makes them difficult and different from restorative feedback.

Step #5: Ask Questions to Gain Understanding

Ask open-ended questions to gain insights. Be sure you fully understand the other person's position. If necessary, paraphrase back to confirm your understanding. Taking into consideration the other person's perspective is critically important. Don't make any assumptions.

Ask the person what they feel caused the problem. How do they see it? How does it make them feel? Ask them what the best course of action should be. The only way to gain a genuine understanding and a spirit of joint problem-solving is through inquiry.

Step #6: Actively Listen and Reflect

Let them talk. Then listen, carefully. Listening is perhaps the most important thing you can do during a difficult conversation. It's seems simple and obvious, but it's rarely done well.

Jane took the new employee to lunch. Each was able to calmly and respectfully state the facts of the interrupted phone call. Each was able to separate the person from the behavior. Each felt uncomfortable that the situation had been magnified by the manager and were relieved to have a direct conversation about what had happened. By listening and reflecting the statements and feelings of the other, they were able to come to a mutual understanding.

When critical mistakes occur, people often want to point fingers and jump to judgments. People get angry. Dealing with feelings at work is complicated and difficult conversations will generate higher than normal levels of anxiety for most people. Expect blame, anger, deflection, or tears.

Recent research[2] supports what many have suspected for years, that emotions are contagious. So it's important not to react, but at the same time you don't want to dismiss feelings.

You need to be in control. Not of the conversation, but of yourself. You'll need to be able to represent yourself in a way that is rational and true to your values. When we're angry, our thinking becomes more rigid and this can block effective communication. So when someone gets angry with you, you need to actively calm yourself. Try deep breathing, slow breathing, sitting back, speaking calmly, and not interrupting. If necessary, postpone the conversation to another time. Don't participate in the blame game, it adds no value and can make the situation worse.

What if the person wants to change the subject? "Really, don't we have bigger issues to deal with than this?" It's important not to disqualify the statement or get defensive. Instead, listen, reflect and evaluate the comment. Then try to move the conversation in the right direction.

If you agree, state that, but move the conversation back to the issue at hand. "I know I've contributed to the problem. We can talk about that. And we should also talk about how you've contributed as well." "Yes, we do have bigger issues to deal with, but it's also important that we discuss this so we can work together to resolve this issue."

If you don't agree, acknowledge what you heard and move the conversation back to the main point. "It may be true that I do the same thing, I'll want to talk with you about that too. For now, I'd like to focus on this."

If the person starts crying, be supportive and understanding. Don't make the person feel embarrassed. If necessary let them sit a bit to collect themselves before they go back to their desk.

Of course, you cannot control the other person's reactions, but you can anticipate them. Along with their words, be sure to observe any changes in body language. Are they still making eye contact? Has their posture changed? These signals help you gauge how the other person is reacting and feeling.

 Quick Quiz: What are the most common reasons that your difficult conversations get off track? How do you keep yourself calm when attacked with anger?

Step #7: Present Alternatives

Usually, the next step is to offer alternatives in an effort to create an action plan. This step should come only after the other party feels they have been heard. In the case of a missed deadline, possible alternatives (including financials) to mitigate the delay or at least minimize further delay should be presented.

After lunch, Jane and the new employee came up with strategies and guidelines to handle their overlapping responsibilities. They agreed that they would meet again in two weeks to see if what they decided was working.

Typically, the goal is to have the other party decide on one of the presented alternatives. In Jane's case, both parties needed to feel like they had some control over the final resolution, so it was best to create and choose alternatives together.

Finally, sometimes it's best to not only let the other party choose an alternative, but also to create the alternatives himself. This way, they are more invested in the solution and are more motivated to change their behavior.

Step #8: Wrap-Up and Follow-Up (Don't Let It Happen Again!)

No matter how the conversation goes, it's always best to summarize in a neutral manner. You can follow the "this is what I heard from you / what did you hear from me?" approach. Here's an example:

"As I understand it, the demo crashed because you were using the wrong version of the database. But, you've got the update from engineering, so you don't think you'll have any issues again. Also, you seemed a bit concerned that this might have an impact on your probation status. What did you hear from me?"

This final confirmation check is very important during difficult conversations, because if the other party has a misunderstanding, you'll find out about it before the problem festers.

Once everyone is clear, focus on the future by clearly stating the next steps. "I suggest that we meet again in a week to see how things are going." It's also a good idea to check in with the person after they've had time to digest the conversation. Be clear that you'll be available for any additional questions or responses as they come up.

Unfortunately, in some cases, that's still not enough. Even if you do view the issue from the other perspective; even if you do prepare for the conversation with experts; even if you are direct and clear; even if you actively listen and provide alternatives—the conversation still may be difficult.

Ultimately if the other party is intransigent, then no amount of preparation will make the discussion easy. Some discussions are just that—difficult!

In this case, you may have to solicit the support of a higher-level third party to force the issue. For example, let's say Jane and the new employee were unable to work out an agreement. The issue might need to be addressed again by the manager.

 Quick Quiz: After reading this chapter, will you change your approach to difficult conversations? If so, how?

Difficult conversations are exactly that—difficult. Ultimately, when a difficult issue is discussed respectfully and resolved, it usually ends up bringing the two parties closer together. The good news is that the outcome of successfully handling difficult conversations is growth and transformation.

The ability to handle difficult conversations impacts the success of a manager, the department, and the entire organization. Failure has a very high cost because issues that fester consume energy and time and negatively impact performance and teamwork. However, when difficult conversations are handled well, productivity, collaboration, and morale goes up. After all, handling difficult conversations is at the core of all relationships.

 Check This Out: Visit www.smarttalksuccess.com /extras for two funny video clips of difficult conversations.

Summary: How to Have a Difficult Conversation

✓ Difficult conversations are difficult for everyone.

✓ How you handle difficult conversations can limit or enable success.

✓ Avoiding a difficult conversation is likely to cause more harm and directly impacts productivity, profits, and relationships.

✓ Follow this process for a positive outcome to a difficult conversation:

1. Consider the other person's perspective.
2. Prepare by understanding your conflict style and anticipating emotional reactions.
3. Prepare by analyzing factors that contributed to the situation and what changes might prohibit the problem from returning.
4. State your observations of the situation simply, specifically, and clearly.
5. Ask questions to gain a better understanding.
6. Actively listen and calmly reflect your understanding.
7. Request or present alternatives for next steps.
8. Wrap-up by neutrally summarizing the conversation and by asking the other person to summarize what they heard.
9. Document and follow up to ensure understanding and change.

Smart Talk Challenge #1

Try starting a conversation that addresses any one of the scenarios at the beginning of the chapter.

For example: You have to tell one of your most productive employees that she dresses inappropriately and unprofessionally. Worse, her personal hygiene sometimes is less than desirable. How do you handle this difficult conversation?

Bad Conversation Starter

"Sue, I wanted to tell you that I've been getting complaints about your clothes. Some people think they are too tight and expose too much of your skin. You know how people can be about that kind of stuff. Anyway, I just wanted to let you know."

Better Conversation Starter
"I'm a little uncomfortable talking to you about this, but if it were me, I'd want someone to tell me. Sometimes you wear clothes that might be better suited for going out at night and that is hurting your professional reputation. You work hard and have great ideas, yet at times I've heard people quickly dismiss them. Sometimes it's difficult for people to see beyond your clothing choices because the clothes you wear don't represent the 'work you' very well. In fact, I think your clothing choices do you a disservice.

"In addition, I've noticed that at times your body odor is a bit strong. I'm not telling you this to embarrass you, I'm only telling you this because I want you to succeed and not let the way you dress distract others from seeing your strong contributions to our company. What do you think? Have you noticed others reacting to you in ways that lead you to believe they weren't considering you a serious professional?"

Smart Talk Challenge #2
Describe how you will handle (or how you should have handled) your most pressing difficult conversation.

Smart Talk Challenge #3
Practice via video or with a trusted advisor the difficult conversation you described above.

Case Study: John B.

My boss has just shared that there have been multiple complaints from colleagues about my attitude. They feel I treat them as inferior; that I'm arrogant, don't value them, and that I wave my management role in their faces all the time.

I've just learned that I recently reduced one valued colleague to tears.

This is all complete news to me—I think my colleagues are wonderful, and value them very highly. The part that really hurts is that nobody thought they could raise the subject with me directly. I had no idea, and now my confidence is completely shaken.

How can I interact with my colleagues in the future without being completely guarded about everything I say?

One suggestion I made to John was to take each person out, off work premises, to have several difficult conversations. He needed to humbly ask each person to deliver to him directly the feedback that he had heard from his boss. I told him that open, honest discussions about difficult topics often lead to much stronger, better relationships even when it feels uncomfortable at the time.

A year later, John wrote me an update:

The first thing to say is that a year on I (and all the colleagues involved) are still here, happily working in the same team. Nobody has felt the need to move on and (more importantly) we're getting on better than ever.

The thing that made the real difference was your advice to talk to each one individually, outside of work. Sometimes this involved going to the local pub, sometimes we simply talked while sharing a lift in the car. It had a real impact.

The funny thing is that I can't even remember now what behaviors my colleagues asked me to change. The thing that made a difference was the fact that I would take the time and trouble to honestly and humbly ask for their advice and feedback, and then take it on board (and pay for the drinks!), that's what spoke to them.

It tore down the perception that I didn't value them. And most importantly, it broke the ice so that, if they have had a problem since, they know that they can approach me directly, and that I'll be grateful for the feedback.

As a footnote (and, in my view the least important part of the story), at the end of last year, the boss who had originally shared the problem with me called me into his office for my annual appraisal. He said that the situation (and my response to it) was not listed as a problem, but as a strength. It was a specific example of something I'd done well in the past year.

So, as you'd predicted, the original bombshell turned out to be good news, although it didn't feel like it at the time! Thanks!

9. Tongue Fu:
How to Deal with Difficult People

Mr. Know It All / Well you think you know it all / But you
don't know a thing at all / Ain't it something y'all

—"Mr. Know It All," performed by Kelly Clarkson

Tom Tenderheart is the CEO of a major widget company. Faced
with lower than expected third-quarter results, he calls a meeting
of his nine top executives. At the boardroom table sit Terri Tattletale, Chris Curmudgeon, Ned Know-It-All, Wendy Whiner, Billy
Bully, Steve Slacker, Paul Procrastinator, Chad Chatterbox, and
Carrie Coldshoulder.

Tom turns to Terri Tattletale and asks her what the reason for
the downturn is. "Don't ask me," she says. "It's Chris Curmudgeon's
job to keep track of that stuff, and he's never in his office!"

"What do you know, Terri?" Chris Curmudgeon retorts. "I'm
always here. It's just that no one ever notices me."

"What's the big deal?" Steve Slacker chimes in. "It's OK if we're
down this quarter."

Ned Know-It-All proceeds to lecture Steve and anyone within

earshot about the importance of company growth and maintaining the bottom line.

"Shut up, Ned!" Billy Bully shouts. "You're such a nerd! No one listens to you!"

Paul Procrastinator says, "I have some ideas about what we can do to boost profits. I'll get working on them sometime next week."

"Nothing ever goes right around here," Wendy Whiner groans. "There's no use trying; we're just going to go bankrupt anyway since no one here knows what they're doing."

Chad Chatterbox sits at the end of the table, talking to Carrie Coldshoulder about his weekend plans and his mother-in-law's bunions. Carrie turns her back to him and stares coldly out the window.

In a perfect world, we would never have to deal with any of these people. However, we don't live in a perfect world and—gasp!— we actually may annoy others too! The sad truth is that no matter where you work, you are going to encounter difficult people. Learning how to better deal with them can mean the difference between pulling your hair out and maintaining your sanity. In the workplace, it can also mean the difference between success and failure.

 Quick Quiz: Do you work with any of these people? Aside from the obvious fact that Tom should probably consider hiring some new executives, what sort of steps could he take to get control of his meeting and get more productivity out of his workforce?

Not sure? Here are some specific and practical tips for dealing with these chronically negative types.

How to Deal with a Tattletale

Remember that girl in the third grade? The one who made sure the teacher knew everything that happened when her back was turned? The one the teacher left in charge when she was out of the room and the one you couldn't stand? Well, now she's all grown up. And she works in your office.

Terri Tattletale is the self-appointed police of the workplace. She spends most of her time talking about mistakes made by co-workers. Unfortunately, she's more likely to tell others rather than go directly to the person because she enjoys stirring up intrigue, controversy, and dissension.

One response to her tattling about someone else is to ask, "Have you spoken directly to Sue about this?" Chances are she will say "No." You then have an opportunity to say, "Well then, let's go together to talk to her." At this point, the tattletale will probably find an excuse to depart the conversation, or make a mental note not to tattle to you again. In a rare case, she may care enough to agree with your suggestion. Any of these results will work.

If you have the starring role in the stories of the tattletale, that can cause an enormous amount of stress. Keep in mind that your conversations and mistakes are the tattletale's ammunition. The best thing to do is to limit your interactions with her (or him) to the essential and professional conversations you need to have. Keep these as brief as possible (and of course, never pass along problems or personal information about other people). If for some reason your boss asks you to explain something the tattletale told her, you can simply say you don't remember it happening that way. Then you should explain it from your perspective.

Quick Quiz: Have you ever worked with a tattletale? If so, how did it make you feel? How did you respond? What might you have done differently?

How to Deal with a Curmudgeon

Long admired by curmudgeons everywhere for their take-no-prisoners approach to hurling surly comments, Muppet judges Statler and Waldorf have insulted everyone from Elton John to Steve Martin—and received big laughs in the process. The problem with real-life curmudgeons, however, is that they aren't funny.

Chris Curmudgeon is bad-tempered and cranky most of the time. He may have had circumstances in his life that cause him to behave this way, and he may just be predisposed to being impatient, rude, and unhappy.

Like with the tattletale, try to limit your interactions with this person, or if possible, just overlook his cranky attitude. (I often will say to myself, "He must be having a really bad day, it can't possibly be me!") Another approach, if it's appropriate, is to try to lighten the situation with humor: "Wow, I'm glad you weren't one of my reviewers . . ."

The bottom line is that you can't change the other person. So, if a curmudgeon attacks you, the best way to respond is to let him have his say and assume his crankiness has nothing to do with you. Listen but don't engage in an argument. The key is not to emotionally react, but instead remain calm. Respond politely, succinctly, and be precise with your language. Paraphrase what you just heard using neutral language: "It sounds like you disagree with X because of Y . . ." Many times the curmudgeon simply wants to be heard, and your paraphrased response might be enough to defuse the situation.

If not, ideally the next step is to find something you can agree on. "It seems we both agree that the goal is . . ." You'll then need to decide whether or not you want to follow that statement with your own point of view. If you are in front of others, you'll likely want to respond by clarifying your position directly (and calmly) to the group. "I chose this method because . . ." If others are not around and persuading the curmudgeon serves no benefit, it's best to simply end the conversation by saying something like, "I suppose we'll just have to agree to disagree."

If the curmudgeon continues on with sarcasm or criticism, don't get pulled in. Keep focused on your succinct response and don't acknowledge their inappropriateness. Don't play their game. They are trying to draw you in so that you feel unstable.

With the curmudgeon the first person to get mad loses. Don't let that be you.

 Quick Quiz: Who is the curmudgeon in your workplace? How do your interactions with a curmudgeon feel? How do you respond? What might you now do differently?

How to Deal with a Know-It-All

You know it. I know it. Unfortunately, we all know it: Ned knows it all. And he knows it better than anyone else.

Ned Know-it-All is someone who prides himself on his vast knowledge of a variety of subjects. He's the annoying guy at work who is always eager to correct your mistakes. You say, "At lunch I'm going to stop at the ATM machine" and his reply is "Well, you know, technically the 'M' in 'ATM' stands for machine so you're really saying it twice!" He may indeed be very smart, or perhaps just a storehouse of useless (or incorrect) trivia. Regardless, he has a hard time participating in conversations without appearing to be a show off (remember the bar know-it-all character Cliff Clavin from the television show *Cheers*?).

I've found the best way to deal with the know-it-all is to assume a curious, subordinate role. Interact by asking "how" or "what" questions. Tap into their vast knowledge. That is a good approach because it feeds the ego of the know-it-all and potentially allows them to change their point of view as they are explaining something to you. I try to avoid "why" questions because I've found that is often perceived as a challenge by a know-it-all.

There's no need to be rude; the know-it-all is annoying but harmless. He just wants others to appreciate his information acumen, so remember to thank a know-it-all for his contribution. Often the know-it-all is desperate for respect, and if you give him some, he may be less inclined to work for it through bragging and attention-getting techniques. It's OK to gently but directly let him know when you've had enough.

A more indirect route to handling a know-it-all is to steer the conversation away from facts and instead focus on feelings or opinions. Interrupt the flow of facts by saying, "Wow, you sure know a lot about printer toner. What do you like about this one?" Then you can jump in with your opinion making the conversation more natural.

Of course, if the know-it-all's behavior is getting out of hand, avoiding this person is useful. But sometimes it's not possible. If necessary, consider finding a neutral third party who is willing to act as a buffer between you and Ned Know-it-All; that way at least you won't have to deal with him directly.

How to Deal with a Whiner

It's truly impressive. The way she can turn any normal word into ten extra bellyaching syllables is extraordinary. And exhausting. Wendy Whiner is never happy about anything. Whereas the curmudgeon is generally just grumpy, Wendy Whiner complains constantly. Whiners are glass-half-empty people. Nothing is ever good enough. You know the type. Whiners are the people who would complain about the seats if you gave them free tickets to the Super Bowl.

The easiest way to deal with Wendy Whiner is to shut her down as soon as she starts. She's usually easy to see coming. She'll stroll into your office with her morning cup of coffee in one hand and the latest memo from the boss in the other. The first thing she'll say is, "Did you see this? What are they thinking now? How are we supposed to do *this?*"

Warning: Whining is infectious! No matter where you work, there's likely to be policies or practices that you don't agree with. Don't be tempted to join the whiners when they complain. Instead, work to be a positive agent for change and help make the most out of whatever your situation may be.

When whiners start, I try to make it a point to be as positive as I can. Sure, I may not agree with the memo, either, but that's not my job. Usually, I just smile and say, "Well, we'll just have to hunker down and do the best we can. Either they'll see it's not possible, or we'll surprise ourselves by what we can do when we work together!"

When you work with whiners, it's important to always focus on the positives in order to contrast the negativity they bring. Eventually, they will either learn to be positive or they will figure out that you don't want to hear it.

Another very effective approach to whiners is to just ignore them outright. It's often said that "the squeaky wheel gets the grease." Sometimes, though, if you don't grease the wheel, it eventually falls off. When whiners don't get the attention they're looking for, they may just go away.

Also, keep in mind that whiners often whine because it's the only they know to seek support. What they're really seeking is someone to bounce an opinion off of or someone who could help solve a problem. They may come to you specifically because of your positivity. If this is the case, lend them an empathetic ear and help guide them toward the solution they are seeking.

VIP Bonus: Download the dos and don'ts of dealing with a whining child. To get this and other exclusive information and benefits join my *free* members-only VIP site by visiting www.smarttalksuccess.com/VIP.

Check This Out: Watch this funny video of *The Whiners* from television's *Saturday Night Live* by visiting www.smarttalksuccess.com/extras.

How to Deal with a Bully

Unfortunately, they're everywhere. They're the ones cutting you off on the freeway. They're the ones posting nasty updates to Twitter and Facebook. They are in offices everywhere. They are bullies, and they don't just roam the halls of schools anymore. The fact is, bullies in the workplace are just as prevalent as they are in the schoolyard. According to a 2010 survey conducted by the Zogby organization, 35 percent of American workers reported being bullied in the office and another 15 percent say they've witnessed bullying at some point in their careers. That means a full 50 percent of the American workforce has encountered a bully in some manner or another.

Bullies spout insults, make threats, and generally humiliate their targets. They like to throw their weight around and have the run of the place. They cause mental and physical stress to their targets and do significant damage to the overall productivity of the organization by demoralizing the entire office. It's hard to get any real work done when you spend the majority of your time walking on egg shells!

Just like in junior high, bullies prey on people they perceive as weak. They build themselves up by tearing other people down. Don't be afraid to stand up to them, especially if they are attacking you publicly. Remember, you're not weaker than them. They just think you are. You don't have to put up with it, so you shouldn't.

If you're the target of the bully's attacks, you're going to need to start documenting. Make sure to include specific incidents and use exact quotes. Telling your boss "he told a really offensive joke about me" isn't going to cut it. You have to let your supervisors know exactly what was said or done and when.

In the United States, bullying is not illegal. Most companies, however, have policies about workplace conduct. From an organizational perspective, it just doesn't make good business sense for there to be strife in the workplace.

Whether you're the victim, a witness, or a manager of an office bully, you have the ability to stop this behavior dead in its tracks. Record specific incidents and bring them to the attention of people who can do something about it.

 Quick Quiz: Have you ever experienced bullying in the workplace? If so, how did it make you feel? Were you the target, or were you a witness? How did you respond? In hindsight, what might have you done differently?

How to Deal with a Slacker

Everybody knows Steve Slacker. He rolls into the office thirty minutes late and takes two-hour lunch breaks. He may be in the cubicle next to you right now. His pants are wrinkled, his hair is mussed, and his shirt is partially untucked. He's probably sitting at his desk with his feet propped up, working diligently on a vitally important game of solitaire. If he thought he could get away with sweat pants at work, he'd probably wear them. Maybe he already has.

There are slackers in every organization. In general, they're bad for morale because their lack of effort and motivation leaves everyone else wondering how they get away with it. Usually, when they put their mind to a task, they do it well. Unfortunately, though, everything about their general demeanor says "I don't care."

What you may mistake for laziness, though, may actually be a failure to understand important aspects about the job. As unbelievable as it may sound, Steve Slacker may simply not know any better.

The first step in dealing with Steve Slacker is to sit him down and discuss his work performance. Take the time to find out how well the slacker understands his job. You may find out that the reason he wasn't doing part of his job is that he didn't know it was actually a part of his job or he may be unclear how to complete the task.

It's important to let the slacker know that when he does contribute you really value his input. Explain that when he doesn't contribute the overall quality of work goes down. You may also need to let him know, gently, that his work up until this point has been unacceptable. You'll need to be able to provide specific examples of where and how he failed to hit the mark. Don't be surprised if he tells you that he thought he was doing just fine all along.

Explain that you'd like a commitment to improvement and discuss consequences for not fulfilling the commitment. If it's a verbal commitment, then summarize his words and send his commitment back to him in writing. With coaching and counseling, hopefully you can help your slacker employee find the motivation he needs to be a productive part of the team. Of course if that doesn't work and the behavior doesn't change then you need to implement the agreed upon consequences, up to and including dismissal.

 Warning: When confronting the slacker, be sure to have documentation ready. They may challenge you on your points. You'll need to be able to counter their excuses with firm, factual evidence.

How to Deal with a Procrastinator

Your team has a huge project due and you have to delegate assignments to make sure everything gets done as quickly and efficiently as possible. The only problem is that one member of your team is a major procrastinator.

When Paul Procrastinator puts off his work, he's forced to rush to meet deadlines, which means his product suffers. Though Paul Procrastinator might be able to fumble through his job, eventually a deadline gets missed or a project is completed poorly. Then, everyone suffers.

Of course you've heard the saying "never put off until tomorrow what you can complete today." I sometimes like to joke that procrastinators "never complete today what they can put off until tomorrow." The problem is that we often think of procrastinators as lazy. Usually, they're not.

You may not think it's important to understand why someone would put off work, but remember this: you'll never solve a problem if you don't know the cause. For Paul Procrastinator, there is usually a number of underlying issues that cause him to dilly-dally. He might be overwhelmed, he could be easily distracted, or he may simply not understand the urgency of the task.

Procrastinators need you to set firm deadlines for them, and they need to hear you make it clear that there will be consequences for not meeting them.

Working with procrastinators will require you to check in on them and ask how their projects are going. You don't have to micromanage here. Every now and then, just ask them, "Hey, how's that report coming along?" or "Do you have any new information for that proposal?"

You'll also want to set milestones and mini-deadlines. This will help break the task up into manageable chunks that a procrastinator will be more readily able to handle. Mini-deadlines will also help you both to easily measure and evaluate progress.

Most procrastinators will probably tell you that they perform best under pressure. This doesn't mean they like to be stressed out, but they do tend to operate better when there's not much time left on the clock. The fact is, procrastinators need a little nudge to keep them going.

To steal a sports analogy, the best way to keep up the pressure on a procrastinator is to treat every project like you're down by 3 at the two-minute warning and you've got to drive the ball 80 yards down the field to win the game.

 Warning: Procrastinators are *not* slackers. You don't need to be forceful with them. You just need to convey the proper sense of urgency.

How to Deal with a Chatterbox

"WILL YOU PLEASE JUST . . . SHUT . . . UP!!" I'll admit it; that's what I really want to say to Chad Chatterbox. He just loves to talk. Put him in any setting, and he's sure to steal the show. Of course, this might be great at a party or informal get-together. Back at the office, though, the chatterbox is much more of a party pooper than a workplace wonder.

A true talkaholic has a comment for everything. He's not necessarily positive or negative, he's just talkative. In a professional setting, he is definitely distracting. What Chad Chatterbox fails to realize is that people don't need or want a comment for every little detail.

As a result, Chad often ends up alienating himself in meetings and a lot of potentially good input gets ignored. Chatterboxes are their own worst enemy. If not dealt with properly, they run the risk of slowing down office communications and productivity.

How, then, do you address the chatterbox? The first step is to tread lightly. Talkative people usually mean well. They're just overly friendly. In their own minds, they're being polite by trying to engage you in conversation. They also typically want to be liked. It's important to be sensitive to their feelings.

When dealing with Chad Chatterbox, do so carefully. Pull him aside and make a joke about his talkative nature. Don't do it in front of other people, but rather keep it just between the two of you. Make it clear that you are approaching him because you care, not because you dislike him.

Believe it or not, knowing when to shut up is a skill that has to be taught to some people. Take the time to show them how to read other people's body language so they can figure out when it might be a good time to stop talking.

The best advice is to help a talkaholic to listen more and talk less. Especially in a sales situation, explain that if he hears "yes" in any form, he should stop talking! Once a person has agreed to something, there is no need to continue convincing them. Chatterboxes often need help understanding body signals so they know when to talk less and listen more. Finally, help him understand how to let others lead a conversation and how this will result in much more productive and interesting exchange of thoughts, feelings, and ideas.

Chatterboxes typically don't see themselves as dominating a conversation. You can help them to learn the art of the give and take by showing them how to share just a little bit of information and then ask the other person what they think. Let them know that when you take the time to listen, people tell you what they want to know.

How to Deal with a Cold Shoulder

I know this may come as a shock to you, but there's a good chance that not everyone thinks you're as awesome as your mom does. That's okay. Nothing says you have to like the people you work with, and they certainly don't have to like you. Sure, it might make the job easier sometimes, but as long you can remain productive, who cares if you're not best friends forever?

You may find yourself in situations where people just don't want to engage you. When you meet Carrie Coldshoulder at work, it can be uncomfortable, for sure. What you have to decide is whether or not it's really a problem.

We may perceive that people are ignoring us when in fact they are not. We tend to make everything about ourselves. That is to say, our first assumption when someone is closed off to us is to think that they're angry or unfriendly. It's much more likely that they have something else going on in their life that has nothing to do with us.

If it becomes apparent that someone does have a problem with you, the best way to handle it is to confront it. Be gentle, be patient, and be careful. When talking to Carrie Coldshoulder, be sure to use open-ended questions. Try asking something like, "I feel like you might be angry or upset with me. Did I do or say something that's bothering you?"

At the end of the day, it's important to realize that if it doesn't affect you or your work product, and if it's not causing a problem in the office, it may be best to just let it go. Continue to do your job and be a positive force in the workplace.

Warning: When dealing with people who are closed off, remember above all else to be careful. It's possible that they may have a hidden agenda that doesn't include you. If they truly are avoiding you, they might be plotting something or angling for your job. As the old saying goes, "Just because you're paranoid doesn't mean they're not out to get you!"

Summary: How to Deal with Difficult People

✓ Ask the tattletale if they've spoken directly to the person they are complaining about.

✓ Don't play the curmudgeon's game. Focus on succinct unemotional responses.

✓ Ask the know-it-all "how" or "what" questions and avoid asking "why."

✓ Always focus on the positives when you are with a whiner.

✓ Document the actions of the bully and bring the actions to the attention of someone who can do something about it.

✓ Be specific with a slacker about how the work has been unacceptable and gain his/her commitment for taking action.

✓ Break tasks into manageable pieces and set deadlines to deal with the procrastinator.

✓ Privately help a talkaholic to listen more and talk less.

✓ To get at the root of a cold shoulder, directly ask the person if they have a problem with you.

Case Study #1: Wael Ibrahim,
Senior Software Architect at Sony Ericsson

"I worked with a colleague who was perceived as a know-it-all. He was a nice person and fairly sharp as well, but I rarely got to say anything in a meeting without being interrupted by him. To make him aware of this perception, I carefully implied it to him once, but he did not gather my meaning.

"On one occasion, I was expected to be on a conference call and it was my turn to present a task that was due but I was not ready. An hour before the meeting, I realized that I would have nothing to say to the group and did not want to disclose the reasons I wasn't ready. Worse, I didn't have enough time to be ready.

"So I invited the know-it-all colleague to the conference call.

"You can guess the rest! Sure enough, he took over the conversation and consumed the whole hour. He resurrected a couple of controversial subjects that got the rest of the group debating with him, and effectively derailed the meeting. Happily this time, I did not get to say a single word, short of announcing his presence. Time ran out, and I got the extra week needed to present the work. Needless to say, I did not invite him to that meeting.

"I subsequently told him the story, and he thought it was pretty funny. But it definitely struck a chord and he became more mindful of his 'know-it-all difficulty' after that."

Case Study #2: Barrett Peterson,
Senior Financial Executive, Consultant, C.P.A.

"My company was acquired by another company. The controller of the acquiring company was an 'intimidator' who liked to yell and pound on the desk to see how you reacted.

He and I spent several days yelling at each other while 'getting acquainted,' following which, we got along very well. It was very primal—two alpha dogs marking their turf. He was a smart executive, capable of substantial charm when he chose to employ it. Many 'intimidators' use this style to 'stress test' your knowledge, confidence, and resistance to pressure, and if you buckle like a lawn chair, you will never recover and attain their respect."

10. Say No More: How to Say "No"

A "No" uttered from deepest conviction is better and greater than a "Yes" merely uttered to please, or worse, to avoid trouble.

—Mahatma Ghandi

Sue's boss asks her to take on a new assignment even though both know Sue's plate is already full. Sue wants to say yes. She wants to impress her boss and show that she can handle the extra load, but it's taking a toll on her life. She's working longer hours during the week and recently started working on the weekends just to keep up . . .

Learning how to say no to your boss, yet present it in a way that demonstrates you are a strong team player, is a skill that many people struggle with. It's difficult to effectively say no. We often don't know how to stand up for what is really important to us. However, saying no is essential to our success.

Quick Quiz: Have you ever taken on additional responsibilities when your schedule was already fully booked? Have you ever accepted a Facebook friend request from a work acquaintance you barely know because you weren't sure how to say no?

From time to time all of us need to say no. In fact, being an effective person (spouse, parent, student, community member, business leader, etc.) means being able to say no. But for many people, that's extremely difficult.

We can hardly blame ourselves for our negative association with the word "no." "No! No! No!" is the stuff of every epic toddler temper tantrum. It's one of our first words we learn as a child and one of the first horrors bestowed on new parents. At work, we really don't want our boss to envision us throwing a childlike meltdown, indicating a lack of maturity. We don't want our boss to see us as selfish children. So we have a hard time saying no. Well, guess what? I have news for you: saying no is *not* selfish!

Repeat after me: it's not selfish.

Saying no is also not an aggressive or negative behavior. In fact, a no uttered correctly is pleasantly assertive. When you say no to something new, what you are really doing is saying yes to your current commitments that are important to you. Think of saying no as a way of honoring your values and existing obligations. If you do say yes, when you want to say no, you need to remember that it was ultimately your choice to say yes.

The ability to say no is actually a sign of professional and emotional maturity. It never does anyone any good to over-promise if you can't deliver. Your business reputation will suffer. And in fact, a well-timed no may even enhance your position. Instead of appearing as if you've got nothing important to do, you're indicating that you are a sought-after resource.

The ability to say no effectively is a skill that's critical to personal and professional success. It's essential for focus and discipline.

Every day, sometimes several times a day, we have to say no so that we are able to say yes to the things that are really important to us.

Why Do We Say "Yes" When We Mean "No"?

So why do we say yes when we should say no? Sometimes we say yes because we underestimate the time it will take to complete the tasks (the new one and the old ones we've already committed to). Sometimes we say yes because in the moment it seems easier, or worse, we don't have the courage to say no. Sometimes we say yes out of obligation or respect for the relationship.

The problem is when we continue to say "yes, yes, yes," we overcommit. I know from personal experience (as I'm sure many of you do, too) that when I'm overcommitted I feel stressed out and tired. And the bottom line is that when we're run down, we're not as effective as we could be and we let down both ourselves and the people we're trying to help.

When Should You Say No?

Keep in mind that some people (like me) will keep asking you to do things until you say no. I often keep piling up requests for people that work for me. I often find myself saying, "It's not that I expect you to do everything, but I'll keep giving you things until you tell me you can't take on any more work."

So the main message of this chapter is to simply say no. Nope. Nah. No way. Never. Uh-uh.

I know, I know, it's a lot easier said than done. So let's break it down.

How do you decide when to say no? There's always going to be some things that deserve your attention and time and some that don't. The problem is that most of us will have more opportunities than time. So again, how do you decide? I devised a little smart talk self-quiz to help evaluate opportunities.

Ask yourself these four questions:

1. Am I saying yes only because I feel obligated or would feel guilty if I said no?

If so, then, surely this would be exactly the time to say no. When we're overly hungry for the approval of others, sometimes we're not aware that in the process what we're really doing is rejecting ourselves. It's important to let go of the need to please others because when you don't speak up about stuff that matters to you, when you stay in deadening situations, when you passively wait for things to change, it drains the joy and meaning from your life.

Life is too short to spend your days not doing what is important to you. Once you spend time, it is lost. So it makes sense to spend your time doing the things that are consistent with your goals and values.

2. Am I saying yes only because an authority figure or expert has strongly suggested I say yes?

This one is a bit tricky. When we are under stress or don't have enough personal knowledge to make an informed decision, we sometimes ask an authority figure or expert for help in deciding. In this case, it is critical to acknowledge that you are under stress and any information you learn should be verified by at least one other expert. Finally, no matter what information you receive, ultimately, you must decide the best course of action for yourself. Ask yourself, "Is saying yes the best course of action for me at this point in time?"

3. Is this new opportunity consistent with my values and does it contribute (or continue to contribute) to my longer-term goals?

There are really two parts to that question. The first part is designed to encourage a review of what is important to you—but more important, it's a reminder to make decisions and to take actions that are consistent with your goals and values.

To remind and reinforce my personal goals and values, I have a sign that hangs directly in front of me that says, "Live life passionately, laugh until your belly hurts, and love unconditionally." I also have pictures of family all around me, again reinforcing and reminding me about what is most important for me.

For work, I keep my strategic goals on a whiteboard and I also keep a clear description of my brand. They are reminders that every decision that I make should be in alignment with my strategic goals and consistent with my brand.

The problem is that we are often inconsistent with our actions. One day we go to the gym to exercise and the next day we slack off. (OK, who am I kidding with this royal "we" stuff . . . of course, I'm talking about myself! I thought about going to yoga and Zumba class today, but I just never got to the gym!) Anyway, the signs I have hanging up are a way for me to constantly reinforce my values and goals and they act as a compass to help keep me on course when I'm making daily decisions.

Then second part of the question, "Does it contribute or continue to contribute to my longer-term goals?" is a reminder about re-evaluation. As we grow, we usually need to do even more to continue improving. So it's important to also ask yourself when evaluating a new offer whether this action is the best way (or still the best way) to advance toward your goals. Just because you did something last year doesn't mean that you should automatically do it again this year. Keep in mind that when you say no to things you've always done, it gives you time to try new things.

And the final question in the "should you say no" self-quiz is:

4. Am I capable of successfully performing this particular task?
To be able to answer this question, first evaluate how much time is involved. Try to be as realistic as possible, taking into consideration invisible tasks. These include preparation, follow-up, and travel. Then consider everything that you are currently doing and how much time you have to dedicate to a new task.

Notice, this is different from asking, "Can I add it to my schedule?" If your available time doesn't fit the size of the task, then say no. If it's important to you, consider alternatives that would still allow you to participate or contribute to the task but on a smaller scale so that it can fit your schedule.

For example, instead of being a club president or vice president, commit to helping with just one activity, such as volunteering to set up chairs before the meeting. The objective is to properly size the effort (again if it is something that is consistent with your values and goals) and say yes only to what you're able to effectively complete.

Think about your skill set. Is what you're being asked to do something that you're good at? If not, perhaps a more effective use of time would be to do something else and politely pass along this task to someone else who is more qualified.

Keep in mind that the main goal of going through this self-quiz is to help you say no. When you know exactly when and why you'll want to say yes, it makes it far easier to say no—and much easier to sustain a no in the face of resistance.

You might be saying, "Well, yes, Lisa, I know I should say no, but I don't want to damage my relationship (with my boss, with my prospect, my father, my grandmother, with my significant other, etc.)." So the key is to learn how to say no without damaging important relationships.

For me, the problem is that when I'm feeling stressed, I sometimes struggle to find the right words. For those times when I'm caught off guard or not really sure what I want to do, I'll say, "Can you tell me more about what you'll need and when you'll need it? I need some time to marinate on your request. Can I let you know in a few days? Does that work for you?"

However, many times, I do know immediately that I'll need to say no. That's when I follow some of the models you'll read about below. I've even practiced and memorized a few of these "no phrases" so that I have a quick, professional response even when I am under stress.

Here are smart-talk models for polite and respectful no's you can use at any time:

Model #1: Yes + No + Yes

Perhaps the most popular model is from William Ury, PhD, author of *The Power of a Positive No* (he also wrote *Getting to Yes* and *Getting Past No*). The first "yes" states what you've already said yes to: "I've recently made a commitment to supervise the new team," or "I really love the new photographs we shot in New York City last month."

The "no" then follows: "Unfortunately, my new team responsibilities have significantly filled my schedule," or "So, I don't think we need to plan another shoot right now."

The last "yes" is meant to soften the tension by showing your concern for the person even though you're saying no: "But I'd love to help you find someone who can fill in," or "But let's revisit this again next month."

Notice the idea is to offer an attractive alternative that still somehow helps the other person. Ury refers to this as "building a golden bridge."

However, there will also be times when you want to not only say no, but also completely detach from the request and not offer some sort of compromise. In those cases, I suggest trying this model:

Model #2: Brief Apology + No + Thank-You

Keep it simple and direct. "I'm sorry. I have a previous commitment, but thanks for trusting me to take on that responsibility." You don't always need to provide a detailed reason—especially if the reason for declining is personal.

A simple "I'm sorry, I can't. Thanks for asking" is not only sufficient, it's better. Just always remember to be polite—not just because it's mannerly, but also because you don't want to damage the relationship by being impolite.

Model #3: Yes + But No

My father used to say, "If something is black, you don't have to say, 'It's black.' You can simply say, 'It's not white.'" In his own way, he was trying to explain that in many situations (and as it turns out, in many other cultures) being indirect is more polite and respectful. So applying this concept to saying no, we end up with the "yes, but no" structure. For example:

SUE: "Boss, can I take this Friday off?"
BOSS: "Yes, you can, but that wouldn't be my first choice."

Use this phrase when you want the other party to suggest a mutually agreeable alternative without having to spell out a specific alternative or, more importantly, without having to outright say no.

Here's another variation on this same structure:

SUE: "Boss, can I take this Friday off?"
BOSS: "Without your feedback at Friday's status meeting we'll fall significantly behind schedule."

Although the boss didn't explicitly say no, he also didn't say yes either. The message is clear: "Please change your plans and attend the meeting on Friday. However, if there is absolutely no other option than your absence, I won't be happy about it, but will figure out a way to get your feedback to the team before you leave."

This works the other way around too. When your boss asks you to do something for which you don't have the time or opportunity, you can say, "Yes, I'd love to do this new high-priority project. Which existing project would you like me to stop working on so I have time to work on this one?"

Here's another option: "Sure, I can take on the new project. I'll just need to readjust the deadlines for my existing projects."

Model #4: Compliment + No

- "Wow, what a great cause/opportunity. Thanks for asking. Unfortunately I'm unable to attend."
- "X sounds like a lot of fun, I'd love to help with Y . . . but I'm unable to attend because of a previous commitment."
- "Sounds tempting but I'll have to pass."
- "Wow. I really wish I could, but I just can't fit it into my schedule."

This approach leaves the door open for another opportunity. The idea is to paraphrase the request in the form of a compliment before going on to say no. This approach emphasizes having the requester feel heard and respected.

Model #5: No + Brief Reason

Sometimes, depending on the relationship, you may want to provide a bit more detail as to why you need to say no. In business this generally boils down to time, money, or skills.

For example:

- "Unfortunately, my schedule doesn't allow it."
- "I am in the middle of several projects and it would be difficult to do a good job if my focus was too divided. I'd rather say 'no' now, than 'I'm sorry' later."
- "Unfortunately, that's not my strong suit."
- "I have no experience with that so it's not a great fit for me."
- "I have every confidence that you/the event will succeed without me, and I suspect you/it will be great!"

(This last one is especially meant for those who ask you to do something when they are lacking the self-confidence to do it themselves.)

Sometimes you'll have reasons that you prefer not to share. Perhaps it's because of the people involved, or perhaps it's because of ethical or moral implications. In this case, don't feel obligated to share your specific reason. It's best to just say, "I'm sorry, I'm just not comfortable with that." If for some reason they press you as to why you are uncomfortable, simply repeat the phrase, "I'm just uncomfortable, sorry. But thanks for thinking of me."

Model #6: No + Brief Reason + Alternative

Just like Ury's model, it's always good to wrap up a "no" sound bite by offering an alternative (if one is possible).

For example, "Thanks for requesting my friendship on Facebook. I also think networking is important. But I'm very keen on separating my personal life from my professional life. I would love for you to join my professional network on LinkedIn. Can I send you a request?"

Model #7: No + My Boss/Spouse/Parent Wouldn't Approve

Finally, I'd be remiss if I didn't include some "just say no" phrases to teach kids. You know, for those times your children might be feeling a bit of pressure from friends to do something they know you as parents wouldn't want them to do.

One approach that I have suggested to my own kids is to blame the "no" on me. "I'm sorry my mom doesn't want me to." Or perhaps for a teenager, "No thanks, my mom would smell the smoke. She's allergic to smoke and is very sensitive to the smell of it."

You can use these same techniques in a work environment.

- "I'm sorry, my boss wouldn't allow that."
- "It's out of my hands."
- "I'll have to check with the powers that be."
- "You'll have to run it by my boss."

Another option is to take a strong stand so that everyone knows just not to ask you ever again. "What are you kidding? No way! Cigarettes do horrible things to your body," or "I can't do that, ever. I find it unethical and inappropriate."

Model #8: No

No matter how old you are or what the request is, Nancy Reagan's advice of "just say no" really does work. Just make sure you say it in a way that conveys confidence and that you don't think the request is a big deal. You might be surprised at just how effective a plain and simple "No, thanks" really is.

Another option for this model is simply to be a broken record by repeating one of the following phrases. "I can't take that on right now," or "Right now, it's just not an option."

Check This Out: Visit www.smarttalksuccess.com /extras for a blast from the past. See the 1980s Just Say No Campaign and a clip of Nancy Reagan's appearance on an episode of *Different Strokes*, plus a 1951 reel on "How to Say No."

Model #9: Evasive No

In some cultures a direct no would not allow the person asking to save face. So instead, an evasive approach is used instead:

- "That sounds really interesting. When can we get back to you?"
- "Is it possible for you to give us some time to discuss and consider this?"
- "We'll call you when we are ready to do that."
- "We'll definitely consider, but our schedule is up in the air right now."

Summary: How to Say No

✓ There's always going to be some things that deserve your attention and time and some that don't.

Ask yourself the following "say no" quiz questions to find out:

1. Am I saying yes only because I feel obligated or would feel guilty if I said no?
2. Am I saying yes only because an authority figure or expert has strongly suggested I say yes?
3. Is this new opportunity consistent with my values and does it contribute (or continue to contribute) to my longer-term goals in my life?
4. Am I capable of successfully performing this task?

How to say no without damaging important relationships:

✓ *Model #1: Yes + No + Yes*

"I'd love to provide a program. But I'm working on my book, so I won't be able to deliver the seminar this month. However, I can do it after my book deadline, which is September 26."

✓ *Model # 2: Brief apology + No + Thank You*

"Sorry, I have a major book deadline coming up. But thanks for asking."

✓ *Model #3: Yes + But No*

"I would love to speak at your event, but it would be very difficult for me to prepare properly with my current schedule. I'd rather say 'no' now than 'I'm sorry' later."

✓ *Model #4: Compliment + No*

"I've wanted to work with your organization for years. I do understand what an incredible opportunity this is. Unfortunately, I'm just not able to do it at this time. Perhaps we can revisit this next year?"

✓ *Model #5: No + Brief Reason*
"Unfortunately I can't say yes, I've got a book major book deadline that I'm committed to."

✓ *Model #6: No + Brief Reason + Alternative*
"I can't because I'm up against a book deadline, but perhaps I can help you find someone else?"

✓ *Model #7: No + My Boss/Spouse/Parent Wouldn't Approve*
"I can't deliver any seminars this month. My publisher wouldn't be happy if I got distracted and missed my book deadline."

✓ *Model #8: No*
"No, thank you."

✓ *Model #9: Evasive No*
"Your event sounds like a great opportunity for me. Give me a little time to consider it."

💬 💬 💬

Smart Talk Challenge #1
Choose three models of no that appeal to you. Work with a partner to practice saying no using each of the three models.

Smart Talk Challenge #2
Next time you are faced with a decision tell the person you'll need to get back to them. Then reread this chapter and choose one of the models to say no. Record yourself saying no and listen back to hear how it sounds.

Smart Talk Challenge #3
During the course of a month, try saying no using all nine models.

Case Study: Ali Brown

"When I started my first business as a marketing communications writer years ago, most of my clients hired me for newsletters, brochures, and sales materials, but I would get the occasional request for something different. At the time I was too naive to consider saying 'no' to any project that didn't fit me perfectly. (Especially when I was living paycheck to paycheck.)

"A perfect example of this was when a colleague named Chip asked if I could write a short script for a customer service training video. 'Wow,' I said. 'Video! That sounds like fun. Sure thing. I'll take it on!'

"Big mistake.

"At first it seemed exciting. But after I got into it, I was miserable. Not only did I spend three times as many hours as I'd planned just on figuring out what they wanted, but I honestly didn't know what I was doing. I'd never written a video script in my life! I thought it would be simple, but it was a whole other world.

"This project not only sucked up all my time, taking me away from my best clients, but it also drained my energy and my confidence. Even worse, I couldn't take on a wonderfully perfect new project that I was offered in the meantime. I lost sleep worrying that I wasn't doing a good job on the project, and worst of all, my fears were confirmed.

"One day Chip left a message on my answering machine that more major revisions were needed. Then it sounded like he hung up the phone, because there was a soft click. But then I heard him start to talk about me with his partner (obviously unaware that his speaker-phone was still on).

"At first I paused the message from playing, because I knew I was not supposed to be privy to this conversation. But I wanted to know the truth, so I listened. My heart sank as I heard things like, 'This writer doesn't know what she's doing . . . we should have hired a real video writer . . . I feel bad, she's trying so hard, but this just isn't getting better . . .'

"So why had I taken on that project?

"This is what we call 'bright, shiny object syndrome,' and it happens to many entrepreneurs. We love ideas and enjoy moving from one idea to the next. We get bored quickly and it's easy to get distracted by something that seems new and exciting. This is especially true when you start experiencing success because it feels as though every opportunity in the world starts falling in your lap. You have to become a master of saying 'no' if it's something that doesn't play to your strengths. That was very hard for me.

"But by sticking with what you know you're good at, you are always confident and calm in your work. You know how to market yourself, and you know who you're marketing to! (Plus you can charge high rates with confidence.)

"So I became very clear at what I'm amazing at, what I offer, who I'm marketing to, and how I want my life to look, so that now, any business or life decision I make is crystal clear. That's the power of knowing when to say 'no.'"

Ali Brown is an entrepreneur mentor.

11. The Art (and Science) of Persuasion: How to Influence Others

I want you to want me. / I need you to need me. / I'd love you to love me. / I'll shine up the old brown shoes, put on a brand-new shirt. / I'll get home early from work if you say that you love me.

—CHEAP TRICK, "I WANT YOU TO WANT ME"

Elizabeth works as an IT Project Manager and has no trouble connecting with her clients and guiding them toward the best path for their projects. But she doesn't have the same success in communicating to the executives in her company. Her communication problem really became apparent a couple of months ago when one of the senior managers mentioned that if only he had seen problem X early enough to implement solution Y, it would have made a huge difference in the company. However, Elizabeth had recognized the problem more than two years earlier. She had brought the issue to his attention and even suggested the ultimate solution. Her advice was not only ignored but its source was also forgotten.

Jeff commutes over an hour each way to and from work. He would like to work from home two or three days a week and on the remaining days he'd like to work alternative hours to avoid rush hour traffic. Jeff's not sure how to convince his boss to approve this change.

Janet wants tablets for her classroom. Budgets have been cut significantly, and besides, no other second grade classroom in her school currently uses tablets.

Quick Quiz: Reflect on the last time you tried to persuade someone of something important. How confident were you with your persuasive approach? How did he or she respond?

What Is Persuasion?

The George Foreman Grill, the Perfect Brownie Pan Set, the Snuggie, the Thighmaster, the Bowflex machine—all of these items taking up space in your home make the power of persuasion clear. Persuasion is powerful. Every day we are bombarded by influence appeals: television, radio, and magazine ads; requests from family, friends, and colleagues; e-mails, text messages, instant messages. Managers use persuasion to convince employees to take on projects, companies use persuasion to convince customers to buy their products and services, children use persuasion to convince their parents to let them see a certain movie. Persuasion is a mission-critical ability to move people from one idea to another and to take action.

For me, the art and science of persuasion is the ability to convince people to freely change a belief and involves understanding how people form opinions and process facts and emotions. In short, persuasion is actively using tactics and techniques to get people to do what you want.

I know you may be thinking, "Lisa, isn't that just manipulation?" My answer is, it depends. There is an extremely fine line between manipulation and persuasion. However, there are important subtle differences. Manipulation is about tricking or fooling someone to do, believe, or buy something that is harmful (or not beneficial) to them and at the same time has an undisclosed benefit to the manipulator.

We need to understand persuasive techniques to protect ourselves from manipulation, but more important we need to be skilled in persuasion to be successful in our daily lives. The bottom line is that people who are skilled in persuasive techniques will get what they want more often. And they don't have to resort to malicious manipulation to get it.

Weapons (or Tools) of Influence

Dr. Robert Cialdini, the internationally renowned expert of influence and persuasion, traveled around the world to study[1] how people exert and react to various forms of persuasion. Through his studies, he identified six "weapons of influence": reciprocity, commitment and consistency, social proof, authority, liking, and scarcity. I prefer to call them "tools" instead of "weapons," but the ideas and principles are the same. These concepts are the tools you can keep in your toolbox to help create the outcomes you're seeking, both at home and at work.

Tool 1: Reciprocity

You've heard the phrase "no good deed goes unnoticed." The fact is, people respect and appreciate favors, especially when they're provided with no strings attached. When you perform an act of kindness for someone, their natural inclination will be most likely to return the favor.

People don't like to feel like they're in debt. When you do a favor for someone, a part of them will feel like they owe you something in return, even if you make it clear that they don't. The concept of reciprocity enables you to lay the necessary groundwork to allow you to wield greater influence later on.

In the workplace, reciprocity means employees expect to earn a paycheck while the employer expects employees to work productively. Treat employees well and they will perform better. Costco

Wholesale Corporation, a membership retailer, is a great example of this. Costco is known for how it treats and values its workforce. In fact, industry analysts have often suggested that Costco should pull back on things like employee benefits. But CEO Jim Sinegal consistently responds by saying that how Costco treats employees is not altruistic, it's just good business because the workers are more productive[2].

Reciprocity starts with being a good boss, a good employee, and a good person. Help your people out. Be the person who comes in early and stays late. Pick up extra duties and do more than your fair share at work. When you do things for others, they will want to do things for you. This includes your boss.

At work, when someone tells you, "Thank you," always respond, "It was no problem at all; I'm sure you would have done the same for me." This simple reply will lay the groundwork for help you might need later on. Through the concept of reciprocity, we gain respect and power. By helping others you are creating an amazing motivation for them to in turn help you.

 Warning: When doing favors for others, do them for the right reasons. Yes, it's possible to reap benefits later on down the line, but if it's clear that you have an ulterior motive, people will resent you for it rather than want to help you later.

To protect yourself from the influence of reciprocity, always ask yourself, "What is the true motive of this person? Why have they offered this favor? Did they make me feel obligated to receive the favor?"

Tool 2: Commitment and Consistency

Research[3,4,5] has shown that individuals will often follow through with an action even after the original motivation has been taken away. When people resolve to do something, they have a tendency to want to see it through. No one wants to appear inconsistent, since that characteristic is generally associated with instability. Consistency, on the other hand, is associated with integrity and rational behavior. Once you get people to agree to a concept, idea, or action, they will likely stick with it to the end. This is also known as the "foot-in-the-door technique." For example, "Would you sign this petition for our cause?" followed a few weeks later by "Would you donate to our cause?" or "Would you agree to re-tweet a few of my marketing messages?" followed a few weeks later by "Would you agree to give my followers a free digital product from you?" followed by "Would you promote my book to your customer list?"

One approach to persuasion, then, is to first get someone to agree publicly to an idea, before asking that person to act in a way that is consistent with the initial idea. For example, one way to put this concept into action in the workplace is at review time. Managers and directors should cocreate quarterly goals and action plans, then have employees formally write up the plans and show commitment by signing them.

Another option to consider when thinking about commitment and consistency as tools for persuasion is to suggest a trial period. This not only makes your idea a little more digestible, but it also sets up circumstances in which you've already gotten them to agree in principle. Once they're on board, even if only temporarily, they will be more inclined to continue with your plan when you ask to make it permanent.

For example, if you are trying to convince your boss to let you work from home one day a week, it will probably be best to ask for a two-month trial period just to see how it works out. Suggest that a re-evaluation can be done at the end of the trial period. Again, if you've already gotten him to agree on a temporary basis, it will be that much easier to make the transition to permanence.

To protect yourself from the influence of commitment and consistency ask yourself, "Do I feel trapped? Have my circumstances changed? Am I still making the right choice?"

Tool 3: Social Proof

Humans are social animals. There is a basic psychological desire to be like everyone else. As a result, we often find ourselves doing the same things we see other people doing in order to fulfill our need to fit in. This is why peer pressure has such a strong influence on us. As individuals, we have a deep, ingrained need to be accepted by others.

Have you ever noticed that when your neighbors have repairs or maintenance done to their home, frequently others in the neighborhood or building do the same thing? A friend of mine who used to sell gutter systems once told me that having work done by one person would frequently motivate others in the area to also want new gutters. Interestingly, he also mentioned that when he sold sunrooms, the question almost every customer asked after inking the deal was, "What color do most other people pick?"

Use your colleagues' tendency to want to fit in to your advantage. Once you've gotten a few people on board with your plan, it will make it much easier to sway the masses. Also, you can integrate elements of social proof by including skillful alignment with outside authorities or even blatant name dropping. No one wants to feel like they're on the outside looking in.

For example, let's say you're trying to convince your product development manager to move forward with plans for a particular product enhancement. You might show how the competition has the feature currently in their product. You might cite a marketing research report showing a market trend toward that type of enhancement. You might also say, "This is the most commonly requested enhancement from the sales team and Bob, our COO, has really been pushing to get this enhancement included in our next release."

Another practical application of social proof is reviews and recommendations. The more positive recommendations a product has, the more likely a new prospect will buy the product. Businesses should encourage genuine recommendations of their products and services and publicly post all reviews. This same concept applies to business professionals. When someone shares a kind word with you, always respond, "Would you consider putting that in writing or posting that to my professional online profile?"

To protect yourself from the influence of social proof, "Was this falsified? Does this make sense? Has there been some sort of mistake?"

 Quick Quiz: Who do you think is more likely to be brought in for an interview, someone who has two or three professional recommendations, or someone who has fifty?

Tool 4: Authority

As social creatures, we crave leaders. We respect strong leaders and acquiesce to authority figures, often unquestioningly. We defer to experts. Generally speaking, we have a natural and strong tendency to follow the instructions of someone we perceive to be an authority, even when we're asked to do the unspeakable. For proof, you need not look any further than the acts committed by German soldiers during World War II or the infamous Milgram experiment, in which subjects believed they were inflicting increasingly high levels of electric shocks to another person (an actor), but continued to follow instructions and delivered more and more powerful shocks, even though the actor was screaming and pleading for them to stop (the shocks were fake).

Of course, you have no intention of committing atrocities and your goals should be more than simply compliance. At work, persuasion is about gaining agreement and making changes to help yourself and your organization succeed. It's about respect and trust. You want people to make changes because you have expertise or knowledge and because you have built a solid relationship over time.

Genuine authority doesn't just come from rank or status. You can assert authority by being the expert in your field or the go-to person for an issue in your company. However, when trying to persuade others based on your expertise, it's important that all parties are aware of your background and credentials. Otherwise you may be unsuccessful.

For example, there have been times when I was not properly introduced before a presentation and I could see from the facial expressions of attendees that they were left wondering, "Who is Lisa B. Marshall? Why should I listen to her?"

In those talks, I had to quickly and subtly incorporate my experience and credentials into my presentation. This can be avoided in any setting by sending out premeeting introductions or biographies that include background and credentials.

In addition to being knowledgeable, an authority also needs to be trustworthy in order to be successfully persuasive. The target of your persuasive efforts needs to know that your motives are to help them and that the information you are providing is objective and unbiased. One way to build that trustworthiness is to be consistently supportive of others and provide useful information time and time again.

But what if you don't have the time? For the answer to that, we can look to advertisers since they introduce new products all the time. What they do is to introduce a possible objection or counterargument against your idea just before making their strongest argument.

The idea in counterargument is to turn against yourself with a phrase such as, "It may seem that . . ." or "You might argue that . . ." Be clear, forceful, and brief when stating the case against the idea. Then quickly return back either by refuting it or acknowledging its validity, but suggesting that it's not a sufficient argument. This slightly more balanced approach helps to quickly establish trustworthiness.

Finally, don't underestimate how much the appearance of authority is influential. It's no coincidence that television commercials sometimes use male and female actors in white coats with clipboards to give the appearance of authority. We defer to authority, sometimes without thinking.

To protect yourself from the influence of authority ask yourself, "Is the authority real? Is this person trustworthy?"

Tool 5: Liking

Interestingly, one of the most important factors in determining a political figure's viability as a candidate is their "likability" factor. In American politics, the candidate that people would rather have a beer with is usually the one who is more likely to win the race. Dr. Robert Cialdini says, "People prefer to say yes to individuals they know and like." This is such an important concept for exerting influence that I more fully expand on it in chapter 14. However, in brief: We like people who are similar to us, who compliment us, and who cooperate with us.

If you want people to align with you, to connect with you, and to be persuaded by you, then it's important you discover genuine similarities, give sincere compliments, and remind others of mutually shared goals. The purpose of these activities is to increase liking on *both* sides. They could like you more from fabricated similarities and compliments; however, the natural result of you finding *genuine* similarities and highlighting positive attributes that you *sincerely* value, is that *you* will feel more connected to that person. And he or she will, in turn, naturally like you more, and thus be more apt to be persuaded by your arguments. Be the person at work who everyone likes. Be friendly, courteous, and respectful. Be likable and charming. I cover exactly how to do that in chapter 14.

Finally, when we are in conflict, we can increase likability and be more persuasive when we remind our conversation partner of our mutually shared goals. For example, once I worked with a hospital to create a procedure doctors could follow when they were at odds regarding a patient's treatment plan. One of the steps I recommended was the following: When conflict arises, stop communicating through the chart and instead make a point of meeting at the patient's bedside to remind all involved doctors of the shared goal—returning the patient to health.

Once you have a mutually agreed upon procedure in place and have secured buy-in, it is important to cue, remind, and hold others accountable to the agreement. At the hospital, it was agreed that the cue words, "Let's press pause" as a verbal reminder of the commitment to the mutual goal of returning the patient to health. The idea was that anyone either involved in the conflict or observing could suggest "I think it's important we press pause." This would signal that the official conflict process should be followed. If there was still pushback, the issue could be escalated: "We all agreed to meet at bedside during conflict. What you just said sounds like you disagree."

To protect yourself against the influence of liking ask yourself, "What if I didn't like this person, would I still make the same decision? Why do I like this person?"

Tool 6: Scarcity

This principle of scarcity in persuasion suggests that if we can't have something, we want it. If something is not scarce, then it's not desired or valued that much. There have been countless studies, including many performed by Dr. Cialdini, that demonstrate people usually react out of fear of losing something more often than out of a desire to gain anything.

Advertisers and marketers use this concept all the time, which is why we see so many "limited time only" offers and ads exhorting us to "hurry while supplies last." Internet marketing professionals often use this principle by making products available for a short period of time at a certain price. Then they take the product off the market and several months later reintroduce it at a higher price, creating artificial scarcity. Other marketers create limited or special editions or limit stock to achieve the same goal.

People are motivated by "loss aversion." That is to say, they want to avoid losing at all costs. When attempting to persuade people, make it clear to them what's at stake if they don't go along with your plan. This should be done gently and with a caring attitude. Remember, we want to be as friendly and nonthreatening as possible. In a sales situation you might say something like this, "If you don't call back by tomorrow at noon, I'll need to cross you off my list. I remember you mentioned this was something that you were interested in doing. It's unlikely we'll ever do something like this again and I just want to make sure you don't miss out." Of course, people respond better when they believe you have their best interests at heart than if they suspect you are being manipulative.

In an office environment, your approach might be more indirect: "If we don't move forward on this idea today, we'll lose the resource that can address this issue, which means we'll have to cover another week of costs until that resource becomes available again."

To protect yourself against the influence of scarcity ask yourself, "Am I caught up in the rush? Have I adequately analyzed this decision?"

Dr. Cialdini's principles of influence provide the foundation to understanding the basic psychology we can use to persuade others. By understanding how we think, behave and react, you can develop the best approach to convince your employees, your boss, your family, and your friends to see things your way.

Taking the Tools Out of the Toolbox

Okay, so these tools are great for understanding *why* people can be persuaded, but what are the steps to take when you want to persuade someone? How exactly do we make that tough sell happen and get what we want?

Plant Seeds and Manage Perceptions

The first step is to set your persuasive goal. What is it that you want to accomplish and how will you be different if you are able to achieve your goal? Having your idea and the benefits of its coming to fruition firmly established in your own mind will ultimately make it easier for you to persuade others. Having a clear picture of your goal is motivational. Once you've got your goal, slowly begin to plant the seeds of your idea.

Persuasion is more effective when it's not a one-night stand but a long-term courtship. In fact, one study[6] showed that even fleeting exposure or minimal conversation before a request lead to higher compliance.

At work, always test the waters before you try to float an idea. If you're looking to telecommute, for example, begin floating the idea early on without coming right out and asking. Say to your boss, "Wow, gas prices are high these days. I don't know about you, but it's starting to get expensive to drive to work! I wonder if anyone's considered working a day or two from home."

You'll be able to get a good idea of your starting point by her response. You haven't asked for anything yet. You're just having a casual conversation. If she puts up a strong objection, though, you'll be able to gauge what sort of battle you'll be facing and will ultimately help you develop a better argument.

Warning: Even if you get a negative response initially, don't get discouraged. It may just mean that you will need to work a little bit harder and a little bit longer to get your way. Try to engage in casual conversations to flesh out all of the objections so you can better prepare your strategy.

Before you go any further, remember your tools of influence, especially reciprocity and likability. Make yourself indispensable. Help your boss and your coworkers in every way you can. Be diligent and punctual. Remember that perception is reality. Do everything you can to create the perception that you are a highly valuable employee in the office.

This reminds me of an episode of *Seinfeld* in which George's car breaks down in his parking spot at work. Unable to afford to get it fixed, he leaves it there and catches rides. George's boss doesn't realize his car doesn't work. He sees that George's car is there early every morning and late every night. The boss assumes George is there diligently working at all hours, when in fact he comes and goes as he pleases.

Of course I'm not saying that you should try to trick your boss by leaving your car at work. What I am saying is that you should be the model employee. By building your reputation and making yourself likable and indispensable, you'll put yourself in a position in which your boss will want to help you later.

 Quick Quiz: What can you do to make yourself more indispensable at work? How can you make your efforts and accomplishments more visible?

Anticipate Obstacles

The next step is to think about things that may stand in your way. What, besides your boss's objections, will prevent you from achieving your goal? Before you present your plan, you need to make sure it will work. In the case of telecommuting, you'll want to make sure your company has the technology and infrastructure in place to make it possible to begin with. Otherwise, all of your efforts will be for nothing.

What's in It for Them?

When you present your plan, you're going to need to show your boss what's in it for her. You will need to present your idea as a means to help the company. Of course, your plan benefits you, but what your boss is going to want to hear is how it benefits your organization.

Any time you are trying to persuade someone, you need to be able to articulate at least three ways in which the other person will benefit from your plan. Think back to your first conversation about the subject . . . you know, the one in which you first floated your idea. Remember the objections your boss raised back then. Use the information you were able to glean in order to gauge the things she cared about most, and make it a point to explain how your idea will make things better for her and the company. You'll want to make your key points several times and support it in slightly different ways each time. Remember to discuss her main objection just before you present your strongest point.

In general, anticipating objections is important. Think about what the arguments against your plan will be, and prepare a rebuttal. Again, remember the initial conversation. Did your boss offer up any objections back then? If so, think about how you can answer them in a way that will alleviate her concerns. When making a logical argument, statistics and research evidence are solid forms of support. It's best to address objections even before they are raised.

What you want to avoid is focusing on how your plan will benefit you. When you are trying to persuade someone to come around to your point of view, you need to remember that it's got to be all about them. It's okay to tell them you'll be more productive or work longer hours because you'll be able to avoid a commute time and minimize interruptions. Don't fall into the trap, though, of telling her you'll be happier or it will save you money. That won't help her, so that argument won't help you.

However, for small requests you may try including your reasons for the request. It turns out that when you make a small request, the word "because" becomes quite powerful. Ellen Langer, a Harvard social psychologist, did a study[7] in 1989 about gaining compliance for a small request: to cut in line for the copier. Her study found that subjects were able to increase compliance by adding a reason ("because I'm in a hurry") versus just asking to cut in the line. Interestingly, when the reason was nonsense but still used the word "because," compliance was still quite high. For small requests, consider coupling that with my favorite form of asking for a small request. "Can you help me [insert your request here] because [insert reasonable reason]."

Use Analogy and Metaphors

Especially when you present a complex plan or abstract concepts, strongly consider using appropriate analogies and metaphors. Compare your ideas with something familiar and simple. Analogies are extremely helpful because your listeners will understand by association. Analogies help people digest complex ideas by comparing them to something they already understand.

Senator Phil Gramm debunked President Clinton's proposal for expanding the struggling Medicare system to include people under sixty-five with this very simple and very effective analogy: "If your mother is on the *Titanic*, and the *Titanic* is sinking, the last thing on Earth you want to be preoccupied with is getting more passengers on the *Titanic*." *Forbes* magazine summed up the power of metaphor by writing "Gramm's response will do more to sink this proposal than will reams of learned, actuarial analyses."

Use Story

Stories are how we connect, change perceptions, and invite others to act. As humans, we are hardwired for stories. Stories are how we make sense of the world and how we learn from other people's experiences.

Think about it. Forty thousand years ago, Togo the caveman hunts the big wooly mammoth and he returns to tell his story by painting pictures on the cave walls. Today, Jon comes back from a big night out at the bars and shares his story by posting gossip and photos on his Facebook wall.

Stories are powerful. If you want to change perceptions or invite someone to act, telling a story is the most effective technique. More important, stories provide a rich context for learning, which means we're better able to remember a story's ideas and act on them or share them with others. In fact, recent research[8,9] suggests that people accept ideas more readily when presented in a story than when presented as facts for analysis.

How Do You Tell a Story?

Putting actions into a sequence is a story. It's that simple.

Ira Glass, who is a master storyteller and the host of NPR's *This American Life,* says a story is a person saying, "This happened, and that led to this next thing, and this next thing and so on;

one thing following another. And some things in the sequence can be: then that made me think of this, and that made me say this."

Always start by briefly establishing a setting, when and where the action takes place. Then introduce the characters through dialogue and actions. It's the characters that interact in the setting, perform the actions, and make decisions. Next describe the specific details of the action (which is often a struggle between opposing forces) and the decisions of the characters using descriptive verbs and adjectives. It does take extra effort to learn how to effectively tell stories, but the payback in persuasiveness is worth the investment. Stories are essential to business success.

For example, if you look back to the beginning of this book, you'll see that I started with a story. The goal of my story was to persuade people browsing in a bookstore that this book would be helpful to them. Go back and reread the opening story to see if you can identify the setting, the characters, the actions or conflict, and the detail through descriptive verbs and adjectives. The more purposeful you are with the elements, the stronger your story will be. What do you think? Was my story successful?

VIP Bonus: Download the PDF "How to Tell Business Stories," as well as gain access to short audios for better storytelling in presentations and other exclusive information and benefits by joining my *free* members-only VIP site at www.smarttalksuccess.com/VIP.

Make Your Request

Of course, all of your planning is for nothing if you never get around to asking for what you want. Careful strategy should be used here as well. When is the best time to catch your boss? Is she a morning person, or would you be better off asking in the afternoon? Think about asking her when you're on more neutral ground, such as a conference or break room, as opposed to her office. Make sure you ask at a time and place when you are sure to have minimal interruptions so that you can have a full conversation about the idea.

Finally, keep in mind that becoming skilled at persuasion requires regular practice and planning. These concepts are ones we need to internalize so that when we are under pressure, we are able to either use this technique skillfully or protect ourselves from manipulation.

Summary: How to Influence Others

✓ Persuasion is when you convince someone to freely change a belief.

✓ Reciprocity means the better you treat others, the better they will treat you.

✓ Gain commitment to a change in behavior before making your request for the behavior change.

✓ Behavior change is sometimes motivated by the need to fit in.

✓ Perceived authorities and experts are more successful in persuasive efforts.

✓ By increasing your likability you can increase your persuasive power.

✓ People are motivated to change behavior through "loss aversion."

✓ Persuasive Process Steps:

1. Plant seeds of behavior change.

2. Manage perceptions.

3. Increase perceived likability and expertise.

4. Anticipate obstacles.

5. Understand real benefits to the other party.

6. Use analogy, metaphor, and story to support your arguments.

7. Make your request.

Smart Talk Challenge #1
Choose one of the opening chapter scenarios. Describe a plan of action based on what you learned in this chapter.

Smart Talk Challenge #2
Think about your most recent successful persuasive argument. Create a story or analogy that would be equally as effective.

Smart Talk Challenge #3
Watch TV commercials with an eye toward tools of persuasion. See if you can name the tools used in the commercial.

Bonus Smart Talk Challenge
See if you can identify the key elements of the story below: the setting, the characters, the actions or conflict, and the detail through descriptive verbs and adjectives.

Case Study: Dr. Robert Cialdini[10]

"This one day outside of my gym, I went to the trunk of my car, where I kept my gym bag. I was carrying my wallet and keys; I didn't even have pockets. So I took my gym bag and for some reason put my keys down and I closed the lid of the trunk. And I said, 'Ack, Cialdini, you just locked yourself out of your car. OK, now you're going to have to go in and mildly embarrass yourself.'

"There was a guy messing with towels and I didn't know him well, but I had been a member of the club for three years and had had hallway conversations with him. I explained my situation and asked if I could use the phone behind the desk. He looked at me and said, 'No.' I responded by saying, 'You don't understand, I've been a member here for three years, you know me.' And he responded by saying, 'No, you don't understand, sir. That phone is for our staff. I let a member use it last week and she was on for forty minutes. My manager told me I couldn't allow anyone else to use it.' I responded by saying, that I don't even have a quarter to make a phone call at the pay phone. And he responded by saying, 'I'm sorry' and returned to the towels . . . I became enraged . . . 'What?

I've been a member for three years and I'm in a fix and you won't even let me use the phone? You've just lost a customer!' I turned on my heels and I stormed out of there . . .

Think about how different it would have been, however, if I had begun with a different context—the context of cooperation. We did have mutual goals. We both wanted me to be happy in that place that ran well. Suppose I had said instead, 'Stan—he had his name right on his shirt)—Stan, I just locked myself out of my car, how can we cooperate to get me my keys?' . . . Of course, he could have made the call for me, he could have given me a quarter, or better yet, lent me a quarter. All of these solutions are vastly better than the one that I chose."

Dr. Robert Cialdini is an expert in influence and persuasion and author of *Influence: The Psychology of Persuasion*.

12. The Art of the Deal:
How to Negotiate

DAVID: Michael, in order to expedite these negotiations,
we are prepared to make you a very generous offer.

MICHAEL: And we are prepared to reject that offer.

RYAN: Michael, you haven't even heard—

MICHAEL: Never accept their first offer. What is your second offer?

DAVID: Twelve thousand dollars.

MICHAEL: Are you kidding me? That is insultingly low.
I don't even want to hear what your first offer was.

—*THE OFFICE*

David works extensively with local elected officials in surrounding communities to identify infrastructure needs (bridge repairs, sirens, traffic lights, etc.) and secures grant money to meet those needs. He used to have daily meetings with local clients and rarely worked in the main District office. However, the price of fuel increased considerably and the District was forced to significantly cut its travel expense budget. Now, most days, David commutes an hour each way to and from the main office.

The cost of fuel has taken a big bite out of David's income. He is thinking about asking for a raise to cover his increased costs, but knows that the District is in a similarly tough financial situation.

He enjoys the work and has a beautiful office with large windows overlooking wooded acreage. He doesn't want to lose this job or antagonize his manager.

 Quick Quiz: How would you advise David to deal with his issue?

There are two ways to get people to voluntarily do something. They can be persuaded to do it, or they can be negotiated with. You learned in the last chapter that when persuading we give reasons to get someone to do something. However, sometimes the other person may not agree with your reasons, no matter how strong your evidence.

Persuasion can fail. That's when it's time to negotiate.

Although the terms "persuasion" and "negotiation" are often used interchangeably, they are, in fact, quite different. Instead of the reasoning you would use in persuasion, negotiators give concessions (e.g., time, money, or actions) to "buy" agreement. Negotiation is like the give-and-take of dance partners; it's a compromise process that requires both parties working together to be successful.

In our jobs, we commonly negotiate price and terms with vendors, suppliers, and clients. With our bosses, we negotiate salary packages, resources, project scope, budgets, and deadlines. In our personal life, we typically negotiate the terms of real estate or car purchases, bank loans, or home repair contracts. Like persuasion, negotiation is a big part of our daily lives.

 Quick Quiz: Think of three things you have negotiated recently in your work or your personal life. Were you pleased with the outcomes of your negotiations?

Why Negotiation Skills Are Important

In my experience, it seems many people are uncomfortable with negotiation, view it as a hassle, or are ambivalent about it. However, good negotiation skills are critical to your professional and personal success. Negotiation is often what enables us to get what we want while making the other party feel good about the outcome.

The same skills that make us good negotiators help us build, maintain, and improve our personal and business relationships, and help us to better understand other people's points of view. Negotiation skills enable us to recognize needs in coworkers, family members, and friends. By recognizing these needs, we become more persuasive.

Effective negotiation skills give you self-confidence and enable you to successfully resolve interpersonal differences in the workplace. Negotiation skills help you meet your needs and also the needs of your employer and colleagues. The same skills you use to negotiate a promotion can be used to make deals with vendors and suppliers, with your lawn cutting service, or with your spouse. The skills that make you a good business negotiator can improve almost every part your life.

Types of Negotiation

Distributive

Distributive bargaining or haggling is also described as "I win-you lose" negotiation. This type of negotiation is usually transactional and occurs when there is a "fixed pie" (a fixed resource, usually money) and the negotiation is to decide who gets how much of the pie. For example, when you negotiate the purchase price of a car, your money is the fixed resource. In this type of negotiation the more you get, the less there is for the other person. This is an older style of negotiating and is based upon very aggressive stances that can hurt relationships. However, haggling is still the standard method of negotiation between shopkeepers and customers.

Warning: In "I win-you lose" distributive negotiations it can be difficult to establish rapport.

Check This Out: Visit www.smarttalksuccess.com /extras to see a montage of great examples of distributive bargaining from the popular TV show *Pawn Stars* and get other exclusive information and benefits by joining my *free* members-only VIP site www.smarttalksuccess.com/VIP.

VIP Bonus: Download "10 Tips to Haggle Like a Pro."

Integrative

However, effective business communicators aim to build trust and foster a continuing relationship. When a relationship is expected to continue beyond the initial negotiation, good communicators choose "win-win" or integrative bargaining over haggling. In this type of negotiation, both sides walk away from the resulting agreement having won something of value. "Win-win" negotiations consider the needs of both parties and are the preferred style of negotiation in a modern business environment.

Going back to our initial example, David now conducts almost all of his business at the main District office in order to reduce the District's gasoline expenditures. Although the District spends significantly less on fuel, David is now using valuable office space in the District office on a full-time basis.

Previously his office was used as a shared space, for several workers. David could try to negotiate to work from a home office instead. This is a win-win situation. David would save money on gasoline and the District could use his office space for other employees. This might be especially attractive to the District since space is at a premium now that more people are working in the office full-time.

Quick Quiz: How could the purchase of a new car be turned from a distributive to an integrative negotiation?

Tips and Techniques for Successful Negotiations

Negotiation is a skill that can take a lifetime to master, but you don't have to master all the techniques and nuances to negotiate effectively. A first baseman can't throw a baseball with the speed and accuracy of the team's star pitcher, but he can still throw it better than an average person off the street. The same thing is true with negotiation skills.

Learning and following the techniques presented below will not prepare you to negotiate arms deals with foreign countries, but they will certainly make you a much more successful negotiator at your job and at home.

Quick Quiz: Think of someone you consider a really good negotiator. What are words you would use to describe that person's skills? Keep these words in mind while you read through the tips and techniques for being a successful negotiator.

Rule #1: Aim High, Everything Is Negotiable

The most important rule of negotiation is to understand that *everything* is negotiable. To succeed, you have to have this mindset. Master negotiators are optimists who expect positive outcomes. I was lucky because I learned this at a very young age. My parents would frequently say, "It never hurts to ask; the worst someone can say is 'no,' and if the person you are negotiating with tells you something isn't possible, don't give up."

Warning: Be careful of *how* you ask for something. It's critical that you ask in a nonthreatening way. It is important to be assertive and respectful at the same time.

To be clear, assertive is not aggressive. Assertive doesn't mean questioning the other person's position. Assertive means continuing to ask for what you want by highlighting the benefits your solution will bring to the other person. It means expressing your wants without anxiety or anger.

Growing up, my mother would often ask and receive discounts in department stores. She would request a discount if a button was missing from a shirt or if an item's packing was dented. If the clerk said she couldn't do it, my mother would say, "Oh, I understand, but perhaps your supervisor could approve that." More often than not, she got her way.

However, the most indelible lessons were when my mother would make friendly conversation with clerks and then in a teasing manner, at just the right moment, she would ask, "Well, since we're such good friends now, do you think you might be willing to help our family by giving me your store discount?" Again, a good portion of the time the answer was yes!

Novice negotiators often don't recognize opportunities for negotiation or give up too quickly. They don't realize that sometimes "no" is not the end of a negotiation. The bottom line is this: When we fail to recognize an opportunity for negotiation, it's nearly always disadvantageous to us. Remember, everything is negotiable.

Rule #2: Do Your Homework

The second most important rule is to go into negotiations armed with information. You have to understand what you want, where to start, when to compromise, and how to close the deal. The more information you have about the other party, the stronger your arguments will be.

Gather as much information as you can prior to your negotiation. What do they need? Get the entire "shopping list" of needs before the negotiation starts. What other options do they have? What pressures do they feel? Who has the power to make the final decision? Who has the power to influence the final decision? How can their negotiating power be countered? What are the traditional customs and terms?

Homework is what helps you to create a realistically challenging starting point. If you start too high, your opponent will go the opposite extreme or perhaps decide not to negotiate at all. If you go too low, your opponent will try to take advantage of you. You want to start with something exaggerated enough to allow for concessions, but is not so over the top that you will be viewed as uncooperative.

When Pat Croce (who was owner of the Philadelphia 76ers basketball team) was recruiting Larry Brown to be the team's head coach, he had to negotiate with Larry's agent, Joe Glass, a seasoned negotiator. Pat had done extensive homework because he knew that six other teams were also competing for Larry Brown. Croce clearly knew that Glass had leverage. Here's what Pat had to say about this negotiation on his blog[1]:

> I thought [the negotiation] was over. After the salary was finally agreed upon, his agent then requested we lease for Larry a 600-series Mercedes and top-of-the-line SUV. Mr. Glass hinted that these issues were deal breakers that would be acceptable by any NBA team. Deal breakers? I wanted to break his bones! But I agreed. Then Mr. Glass raised another issue—he requested that Larry be compensated for any loss in value of his Indiana home when he sells it to move to Philadelphia. My hands were tied. I surrender, stop! He didn't. His parting question was one I remember distinctly: "Obviously all of Larry's moving expenses will be covered?" It was a question with only one answer. Obviously!

Doing your homework is easier said than done. Even an experienced negotiator like Pat Croce can run into trouble if he doesn't have a rock-solid plan with all the information up front, or doesn't have all the information when finalizing the terms of the deal.

Rule #3: Show How the Other Party's Needs Will Be Met

Always consider the other person's point of view and think about what that person really needs to take away from a negotiated agreement. Remember that satisfaction means that other person's interests have been met.

Let's get back to David's dilemma.

On a superficial level, the District for which David works needs a grant coordinator. Trying to negotiate a raise simply because he is a grant coordinator is pointless because David is already doing the work. If he were to leave, the District would simply hire a replacement.

On a deeper level, the company needs more than just someone to coordinate grant projects. The company needs someone the local elected officials know and trust. They need a person who has a strong working relationship with the funding agencies, who can explain why placing a tornado warning siren in a small town in their District is more important than a bridge repair project in a neighboring District. The District needs employees who are willing to "go the extra mile" to make projects happen, and who are concerned not just with earning a paycheck, but with the success of the Development District as a whole.

Understanding these needs and showing how his proposal satisfies them all are crucial aspects to David's successful negotiation.

Rule #4: Never Negotiate Without Options

Successful negotiators go into every negotiation with a prioritized list of goals. Some of these items are actual needs that must be met before a deal can be struck. Others are concessions that it would be nice to have, but which the negotiator can do without if it is necessary to move a settlement forward. Effective negotiators are flexible, always looking for a possible compromise, and are open to a range of fair solutions.

A person who goes into a negotiation with no options is in a very weak position. Good negotiators are willing to walk away from the deal if they cannot reach an equitable agreement.

The unsavory auto mechanic on a long stretch of desolate road can charge whatever he wants to replace a radiator hose. He knows that if you need a new hose for your car's cooling system, he is your only option. You won't be able to drive to the next town without circulating cooling fluid. Alternative solutions allow you to bargain in a negotiation, or even walk away, but not in the mechanic's case because you have no other option.

Rule #5: Know Your Best Alternatives to a Negotiated Agreement

A crucial part of negotiation preparation is to determine what's referred to as your Best Alternative to a Negotiated Agreement (BATNA). This is the course of action that could be taken if the negotiations fail. In general, you shouldn't accept a solution that is worse than that. Knowing your best alternative to a negotiated agreement is an incredibly powerful tool.

For example: David's best alternative to working from home might be to purchase a more fuel-efficient vehicle. He incurs a debt, but his monthly car payment of $300 would allow him to reduce his fuel usage to $250 dollars per month. In total, David would be spending $550 instead of the $600 he is spending now. Knowing that his best alternative will save him $50 per month, David is able to value any counteroffer to his proposal appropriately.

Rule #6: Suggest Equal Alternatives

We've already mentioned that options are essential to a successful negotiation. Another great approach is to suggest two or three alternatives that are of equal value to you. By suggesting multiple resolutions, you show that you are a reasonable person. The multiple suggestions indicate flexibility and your willingness to negotiate. Tie these suggestions to the company's objectives to demonstrate that their needs are being met.

Let's think about David's situation and consider some alternative resolutions that would all be of value to him. The ideal outcome for David would be a $7,200 raise. This would cover his $600 per month fuel costs. He could offer to handle additional projects to provide the District with more value in return for that raise.

He could also offer to use shared office space in his own town. He could probably rent the space for less than he is spending on fuel to commute to and from work each day. Even if the savings to him were small, he would also be gaining an extra two hours of personal time each day by eliminating the commute. He could even argue that this solution is eco-friendly, because it eliminates his vehicle from the roads for two hours each day, and that it would benefit communities close to his town.

Finally, he could offer to work from home. He might even offer to use his personal cell phone for business at no charge to the District. With this solution, the District would be able to utilize his space for another employee and also save money on office supplies and utilities because David would be using his own electricity, printing supplies, and phone.

Rule #7: Open the Lines of Communication

David is a conscientious grant coordinator. He does good work and is happy in his position. He is presenting a proposal only to cover his increased fuel expenses as a result of the change in District policy. These are all things that he needs to communicate to the District Director. If he simply asks for a raise, the Director may think he is unhappy with his job or his salary. Communication is essential to good negotiation.

If you are unable to effectively communicate with your opponent, then no negotiation can take place. You have to first have an open line of communication. Effective communicators always use diplomatic communication to build rapport and nurture relationships. They do this because of the reciprocity norm of human behavior. If you are trustworthy, reliable, and fair, your opponent will likely reciprocate and treat you in the same way (read more about this in chapter 11).

When presenting your proposal, encourage the other person to reveal their needs by asking questions such as: "What has been your experience with . . . ?" "What is most important to you? Why?" "What resolution would you suggest?"

If you are finding it difficult or impossible to open lines of communication, consider another route. Engage a third party (e.g., a colleague, a professional mediator, or your client) who you know has a good rapport with your opponent (or someone on your opponent's team).

Rule #8: Challenge the Validity of the Other Side's Arguments

Once you receive your opponent's information, you'll need to challenge the validity of their statements. Again, be assertive, not aggressive. Challenge in this case means that you should be thinking for yourself and not just accepting what the other side tells you. You have the right to question things such as price, standard language, and policy. You need information so that you are able to make up your own mind, as opposed to believing everything you are told.

Quick Quiz: Think of some statements that were presented to you in a negotiation that you did not question, but which later turned out to be inaccurate. Would questioning the validity of those statements have changed the way you negotiated the agreement?

Rule #9: Listen and Modify Alternatives

Once you have presented some alternative resolutions to the issue, listen to what the person has to say about them. The director may be amenable to some parts of David's suggestions but resistant to others. By carefully listening to the responses, watching body language, making eye contact, and using all the other good communication techniques that he knows, David may be able to construct other alternatives to blend together the acceptable portions of several different potential resolutions.

By listening to his boss, he may be able to open the discussion to concessions he had not originally considered. Perhaps, in lieu of a raise, David might gain the use of the company vehicle. He might discuss increased benefits, like additional vacation days or an accelerated rate of vacation time accumulation. These things all have value, and successful negotiators are always willing to consider alternatives with an open mind.

Rule #10: Manage Perceptions

Good negotiators also plant seeds to manage the perceptions of the other person. When you open the negotiation, always ask for some things that you would like to have but which are not crucial to your position. These things would be beneficial to you, but they may also be beneficial as concession points later in the negotiations. Giving them up later allows the other person to walk away from the negotiation feeling like they scored a "win."

Rule #11: Avoid Early Commitments

In most cases, it is best to avoid any early commitments. Every concession we grant early in the negotiating process strengthens the other person's bargaining position. We are negotiating for an integrative resolution, and that means that the needs of both parties will be met in some measure.

A distributive negotiator would advise us to never give up something without getting something in return. To a certain extent, that is also good advice in the integrative point of view. But the key difference is that in a win-win situation, we *offer* to give something in return for something. Giving something up and then asking for something in return is not nearly as effective.

Rule #12: Keep Discussions Positive

Remember, you are seeking to show how the other person's needs are being met along with your own. There are always possibilities of negative outcomes, but it is important to let the other person see that you have a positive outlook by using positive language. This encourages optimism in the other person, too, and reassures the other party that the negotiation can be concluded with positive outcomes for both sides. This outlook makes it much easier for the other person to reach agreement with you. Forcing the other party to "lose" the negotiation creates anger and resentment that can become impediments to your goals. Positive language is crucial not just in negotiations, but in all communication. Read chapter 13 for more.

Rule #13: Have Patience

Always negotiate with patience. Patience shows the other person that you are under no pressure to rush into a decision, and that you will carefully consider every counteroffer. Of course, we are all usually under some pressure to conclude a negotiation, but it is essential that we realize that the other person has very similar pressures. Patience usually increases pressure on the other party. This may prompt the offer of additional concessions.

Rule #14: Manage Anger

Don't take anything personally. Negotiations can often become heated. It is important to remain open to possibilities and to think clearly. Anger usually makes us react without thinking, and that is a bad tactic in a negotiation. Taking frequent breaks is a good way to step back from the situation, relax, and visualize the negotiation objectively, without emotion.

Summary: How to Negotiate

✓ Negotiation skills rely heavily on communication and provide benefits beyond the ability to negotiate effectively. They make you a more confident all-around communicator.
✓ After persuasion fails, negotiation is the next approach to gaining an outcome.

✓ Distributive bargaining is "I win-you lose," while integrative bargaining is a "win-win" for both sides.

✓ Integrative negotiations consider the other side's needs and foster continuing relationships.

✓ Everything is negotiable.

✓ Go into negotiations armed with information.

✓ Meet the other side's needs.

✓ Never negotiate without options.

✓ Know your best alternative.

✓ Challenge the validity of all information presented.

✓ Consider opposing points of view.

✓ Suggest alternative resolutions that are valuable to you.

✓ Really listen to what the other person has to say.

✓ Ask open-ended questions.

✓ Keep the discussions positive.

✓ Always negotiate with patience.

✓ Avoid any early commitments.

✓ Manage the perceptions of the other side of the bargaining table.

✓ Manage your emotions.

Smart Talk Challenge #1

In your next negotiation at work, create and offer three equal alternatives and see how the other person reacts.

Smart Talk Challenge #2

Prepare a plan to negotiate a pay increase following the guidelines of this chapter.

Smart Talk Challenge #3

Imagine you are a very young professional and because your boss had a sudden heart attack, you have been promoted into your first management position on a temporary basis. Your boss never returns to work and you are given the position permanently. You've now been the manager for two years. You've received small increases, but never any significant bump up in salary. When you were moved to permanent status, your new boss wanted to wait to see how things worked out. Prepare a negotiation plan.

Case Study: Warren Buffett

In 1955, two textile manufacturing companies merged: Berkshire Fine Spinning Associates and Hathaway Manufacturing Company. After the merger, Berkshire Hathaway was controlled by a man named Seabury Stanton. The company initially operated fifteen production facilities and generated over $120 million in annual revenue. During the next five years, Stanton began closing facilities and put thousands of people out of work.

These drastic layoffs and closures showed as large profits in the accounting records, and the company stock value increased after each plant closing. An investor named Warren Buffett noticed the trend in stock value and in 1962 began buying stock in Berkshire Hathaway. It turned out to be a bad investment. Within two years it became clear to Buffett that the United States textile industry was floundering, and that stock increases based on plant closings could not continue indefinitely with only eight plants left open.

He negotiated with Stanton to sell back stock, and in 1964 Stanton offered to buy back Buffett's shares at a price of $11.50 per share. Buffett was happy to agree. However, when the formal paperwork was sent over to his office, Buffett saw that Stanton had tried to lower the purchase price. The paperwork listed $11.375 per share instead of $11.50.

Buffett became angry at this deception, and instead of selling his shares he instead purchased additional stock. He took control of the failing company and his first action was to fire Seabury Stanton. In 1967, Buffett expanded the company into insurance holdings, and three years later acquired an equity stake in GEICO, the Government Employees Insurance Company. Berkshire Hathaway is now the eighth largest public company in the world, and its stock was selling for $108,020 *per share* in September 2011.

This story could be read as a lesson in ethical negotiation. If Seabury Stanton had not attempted to cheat Warren Buffet, he would have shared in the tremendous wealth that Berkshire Hathaway has generated. However, Buffett reacted in anger to Stanton's ploy. Although it would seem that he came out all right in the end, Buffett disagrees.

In an October 2010 interview[2] with CNBC, Buffett described the transaction as "the dumbest stock I ever bought." He estimates that, had he invested the same money directly into the insurance industry, he would have earned several hundred billion dollars more than the money he has received from one of the most successful companies in the world.

13. Say Yes to Impress:
How to Use Positive Language

You've got to accentuate the positive / Eliminate the negative / Latch on to the affirmative / Don't mess with Mister
In-Between

—JOHNNY MERCER, "AC-CENT-TCHU-ATE THE POSITIVE"

ACCORDING TO OUR RECORDS, YOU ARE INELIGIBLE FOR
ANY TAX REFUND BECAUSE THERE ARE TAX PERIOD (S) FOR
WHICH YOU ARE LIABLE BUT HAVE NOT FILED.

I once received this letter from the City of Philadelphia. Notice the
negative language: "ineligible," "liable," "not filed." Even the capital letters contribute to the feeling of negativity. Negative language
often has a subtle tone of blame. It tells the recipient what can't
be done, but doesn't tell the recipient what can be (or has been)
done. Negative language also conveys a poor image to customers.

Now contrast the letter with the one I rewrote for them:

Thanks for filing your 2010 business privilege tax return. Please
provide proof of payment for your 12/31/2008 return and we can
promptly send your requested refund.

Instead of putting people on the defensive, positive language shows a willingness to help. It's the same information, but presented in an upbeat, helpful tone. (And no, I don't expect the government to change their language, I just thought it was a good example! I'm still waiting for my refund.)

My point is that if you want to move toward more positive communication, the first step is to identify and eliminate negative phrasing. I cringe every time I hear someone say, "Oh, I'm a terrible public speaker" or "I hate networking," or when I hear a manager say, "Oh, he's not creative at all," or when I hear a parent say, "Oh, she's not good at math." By using negative words, the only thing we are doing is setting limits. However, it's very easy to fall into a negative language pattern and often we're unaware of it. Remember people will very quickly make a judgment about you based on the words you choose.

 Quick Quiz: Listen to what you are saying about yourself and others. Are you using primarily negative or positive words? Do you notice a difference in the way people respond to you?

A single thought can be communicated in a variety of ways, each time revealing completely different emotional connections. For example, what if someone called you "stingy" instead of "frugal," or "nitpicky" instead of "meticulous," or "headstrong" instead of "determined." (And yes, I chose those particular words because they have been used to describe me.)

Imagine your boss telling you, "You made a bad decision." Would you feel differently if he said, "You might want to reconsider that"? What if in response to a new idea, your boss says, "That will never work" when instead he could have said, "Can we explore some alternatives?"

My father was an expert at this. I remember one time when I was about six years old he said, "Honey, would you mind running upstairs to get my socks?"

"Yes, I would mind," I said cheekily.

He responded by saying, "Oh, that wasn't a request, I was being positive and polite. When I ask you to do something, I expect you to do it."

I never, ever forgot that lesson.

Here are a few more of the positive expressions I learned from my dad:

- Instead of "That's a lie," he would say, "I find that hard to believe."
- Instead of "You're stupid," he would say, "You are smarter than that."
- Instead of "Stop running," he would say, "Please walk."

He didn't want to be a nag, instead his goal was to be my coach. It seems so simple, so obvious, yet, like the letter above demonstrates, it's not easy to turn our language patterns around. It takes thought and effort to break career-long habits. It's why senior managers often encourage employees to use the word "challenging" instead of "difficult," or "challenge" instead of "problem," or "opportunity" instead of "issue."

A single change in word choice can make a major difference in perception. A great example of this was when Richard Nixon famously declared to an Associated Press managing editors conference that "people have got to know whether or not their president is a crook. Well, I'm not a crook." By repeating the negative language, his words immediately made everyone think of him as a crook.

 Quick Quiz: What positive and negative expressions do you regularly use? How do you think your words are perceived?

In general, negative words have a negative influence of which we are often unaware. I am guilty of this myself. In fact, someone once suggested that I was a "Negative Nancy." I demanded examples (notice I could have *asked* for examples). He pointed out that instead of saying "yes" I sometimes use substitute words such as "sure," "OK," and "yeah."

"Yes" and "Sure" Are Not the Same

You're probably wondering "What's the big deal if Lisa says 'sure' instead of 'yes'?"

Well, he argued that the other words really aren't the same as "yes." He said, "Lisa, when you say 'yes' it's crystal clear that you mean yes, but when you say 'sure' or 'OK' or 'yeah' it's like you are reluctantly agreeing. It's even worse when you say 'whatever.'"

I had to admit, he had a point. After listening more carefully to my word choice, I realized there is a slight but perceptible difference, especially when the words are delivered in a negative tone of voice.

Tone Matters

One day a lisabmarshall.com sales representative asked, "Lisa, can I get an external mouse?" I could have responded by saying, "Yes, absolutely." Instead I heard myself sigh "Okay."

I was communicating reluctance. In this case, I was thinking, "There is a trackpad on the laptop, so do you really need a separate mouse?" Earlier in the week I had suggested he give the trackpad a try and if he didn't like it, I'd consider buying an external mouse. So in essence, I had already said yes. It definitely would have been more positive for me to respond by saying, "Yes, absolutely." And I could have even said that with a smile on my face.

Yes, But . . .

Later that same day, the sales rep said, "How about we run a contest?"

I heard myself reply, "Yes, we could but . . ." I'm sure you've heard that "yes, but" is the equivalent of saying "no." As soon as I heard myself say "yes, but" I backtracked.

"Wait, wait, wait, let me try that again." I had to remind myself to use "yes, and . . ." instead of "yes, but."

So, here's what I said instead:

"Yes, I think having a contest is a good idea. And when we have the resources to administer it properly, we will definitely do that."

 Warning: "Yes, but" is a very thinly disguised no, which discredits the other person's idea and potentially leads to unhealthy conflict. By the way, the same goes for "yes, but's" cousin, "yes, or."

"Yes we could run a contest or we could try using a coupon code." At least an alternative is suggested in this case, but it still negates the original idea.

Using these sort of subtle negative words creates conflict and confrontation where none is necessary.

Don't Be a Yes-(Wo)Man

However, to be clear, I'm not suggesting that you gratuitously just say yes to everything, either. For a business to be successful, you need healthy conflict to arrive at good solutions. Being a yes-man—or in my case, a yes-woman—doesn't work.

 Warning: Agreeing just to avoid conflict is equally unproductive.

A "yes, and . . ." approach allows you to work through conflict in a positive manner. You can "yes" to parts of an idea and then express your concerns about the parts you disagree with. The point is to first mention what you agree on in order to find common ground. By speaking to the commonalities first, you build a strong foundation, which then opens the door for a healthy discussion of the disagreement.

"Yes, and . . ." sets the stage for healthier, more effective communication. It helps create an environment that encourages discussion of ideas. It moves us forward.

Beware of Negative Accusations, Statements, and Questions

When confronted with an accusation, be careful not to latch onto the negativity, but instead respond with positive, declarative language. Don't fall into the trap of repeating the original negative allegation. It will just perpetuate the claim and reinforce the strength of the accusation.

For example:

When you hear: "Isn't your project running over budget and behind schedule?

Don't say: "No, my project isn't running over budget and behind schedule."

Respond positively: "The project is still scheduled to complete on time and on budget."

When you hear: "Is your project negatively affecting the environment?"

Don't say: "No, our project is not negatively affecting the environment."

Respond positively: "The environmental impact for this project will be minimal, if not zero."

When you hear: "Are you going to be late?"
Don't say: "No, I'm not going to be late."
Respond positively: "I plan to be on time."

Similarly, when asked a question, don't respond negatively by saying "what isn't," instead respond positively with "what is."

When someone asks: "How are you feeling today?"
Don't say: "No complaints."
Respond positively: "I'm excited and ready to get started."

When someone asks: "What do you think about my idea?"
Don't say: "Not bad."
Respond positively: "Sounds interesting."

When someone asks: "Can I do . . ."
Don't say: "I don't have a problem with it."
Respond positively: "Yes, you may."

Finally, when asking a question, frame it positively.
Instead of: "Why don't we meet on Tuesday?"
Ask positively: "Let's meet on Tuesday."

Keep in mind that positive framing conveys what you are for, not what you're against. It says what you are going to do, rather than what you're not going to do, what you can do rather than what you can't do.

Don't Use Absolutes

Absolutes like "never" and "always" are rarely true and generally just exacerbate a situation. "You are always late" or "You never contribute in status meetings" or "Take it or leave it." These words are often used to criticize or attack others. Or worse, the receiver may choose to ignore the message altogether thinking it's just an exaggeration. Instead of absolutes, use words like "often" or "seldom" in your communication.

Along the same lines, avoid negative phrases like, "I can't," "It's impossible," "This won't work," or "I'll try." Instead substitute neutral words, "This is a real challenge" and then figure out if it is indeed possible.

Similarly, stay away from "should have" and instead use "could have." "You should have completed the attendee list before you started on the next project." Contrast that with "You could have completed the attendee list before you started on the next project." The second statement is much gentler and less accusatory.

Avoid Complaining, Griping, and Using Profanity

At work, no one wants to hear about your personal problems. In addition, there is no reason to complain about things over which you have no control, such as your customers or the economy. And of course, don't swear. Complaints, gripes, and swear words should be filtered out from your vocabulary to remain positive. Instead focus on what you can learn from a situation. "I could have handled that customer situation better. Next time, I'll try to . . ."

Don't Accuse Someone of Lying

Inevitably, there are times when we notice that the word or promises of others seem to have changed, either through fibbing or forgetting. The best way to handle this in a positive manner is to resist the urge to say, "But that's not what you said . . ." or more blatantly, "You're a liar!" It's best to simply state what it is that the person originally said. Of course, even better, if you have a record to produce as evidence (either written or recorded).

Similarly, banish the words, "to be honest" or "let me be honest with you" from your vocabulary. Immediately, most people will think, "Have you been lying to me up to this point?" These phrases are not positive and can significantly damage your credibility.

To be clear, using positive language does not mean skipping through the office bright and bubbly, oblivious to conflict and difficulties. However, if you consciously use more positive language, you'll begin to see differences in your life. Just remember the words of Mahatma Gandhi:

Keep your thoughts positive, because your thoughts become your words.

Keep your words positive, because your words become your behavior.

Keep your behavior positive, because your behavior becomes your habit.

Keep your habits positive, because your habits become your values.

Keep your values positive, because your values become your destiny.

There is no doubt that the language you choose can make a *huge* difference in your life! Our word choices communicate feelings and thoughts and become reality. They reveal our attitudes and they create relationships with the people around us. Positive words are powerful (and smart)!

Summary: How to Use Positive Language

✓ Positive expression of thought is motivational.
✓ Negative words have a subtle negative influence.
✓ Use "yes" rather than "sure" or "yeah."
✓ Use a positive tone.
✓ Use "Yes, and . . ." instead of "Yes, but . . ."
✓ Respond to negative accusations using positive words.
✓ Don't use absolutes, like "never" and "always."
✓ Avoid negative phrases such as "I can't" or "It's impossible."
✓ Use "could have" instead of "should have."
✓ Avoid complaining, griping, or using profanity.
✓ Don't accuse someone of lying.

Smart Talk Challenge #1
Write down the top ten negative phrases you typically use. Then create their positive equivalents.

Smart Talk Challenge #2
Read this list of twenty-five negative adjectives and see how it makes you feel: arrogant, belligerent, boastful, bossy, callous, cantankerous, compulsive, cynical, deceitful, dishonest, domineering, greedy, impatient, inconsiderate, intolerant, irresponsible, jealous, narrow-minded, obsessive, patronizing, pompous, pusillanimous, quarrelsome, quick-tempered, ruthless.

Now read this list of twenty-five positive adjectives and see how it makes you feel: ambitious, bright, charming, cheerful, dazzling, decisive, delightful, dynamic, enthusiastic, exuberant, fantastic, industrious, plucky, responsible, self-assured, shrewd, sincere, smiling, stimulating, successful, talented, vivacious, wise, witty, wonderful.

Smart Talk Challenge #3
For one week, instead of saying "thank you" or "no problem," try saying "it's my pleasure."

Case Study: Ritz-Carlton Hotels

Ritz-Carlton Hotels is a collection of world-class luxury hotels. One noticeable difference between these hotels and others is positive language. Every employee learns about the corporate culture, philosophy, and language in their "Legendary Service" training session. They are taught to say, "It's our pleasure," instead of "You're welcome" or "No problem" whenever they are thanked for a service or favor. They do this because they know that this positive language causes a ripple effect. It makes the employees optimistic, which in turn makes customers optimistic, and that creates an extremely pleasant atmosphere.

14. Magically Delicious:
How to Unleash Your Inner Charisma

The charm of you is comparable to a Christmas tree with
toys, / With little girls and boys when first they see the tree.

"The Charm of You," performed by Frank Sinatra

John works at a company with a notoriously stingy office manager. His coworkers often joke that she treats every request for office supplies as if it were coming out of her own personal stash.
Most people hate to deal with her, so much so that some even buy
whatever they need with their own money. Not John.

He simply asks and receives. Why? Because John is charming
and likeable. John once told me, "You have to put money in the
bank in order to get money out." Of course, he wasn't talking
about cash, but about a certain kind of richness. Richness in the
quality of the personal connections he makes.

John makes it a point to stop by the offices of his coworkers
and check on them.

He spends extra time connecting with them, asking about
their weekend or their family or whatever is important to them.
He makes an effort to care about the people around him. He con-

sciously chooses to make sincere and genuine "charm deposits" because he understands the importance and value of putting others first. And the bonus for him is that he gets to enjoy the dividends of charming likability.

Quick Quiz: Have you ever met someone who has an irresistible magnetic force? What traits and characteristics do the charming people you know have? How are they different from others? How do you feel when you spend time with genuinely charming people?

What Is Inner Charm?

John exhibits what I call "inner charm" or "authentic charisma." Charm is, by definition, "a quality of pleasing or delighting, to attract strongly or irresistibly." For me, however, both charm and charisma are equal to likability. Charmers are brilliant communicators. Some might even say, they're just short of magic! It's a special almost indefinable quality that leaves you feeling wonderfully energized after spending time with that person. John is one of those people. Psychologist Ronald Riggio[1] believes charisma includes: expressivity, sensitivity, control, eloquence, vision, and self-confidence.

But sometimes people view charm with a slightly negative connotation, as if charm is somehow superficial or manipulative. Yet John is an authentically friendly person and really does sincerely care about the people around him. There is nothing manipulative about John's charm. It is ethical and authentic, and it's so powerful that others are naturally drawn to him and instinctively have a desire to interact with and support him because he makes them feel good about themselves. I mentioned this in chapter 11, but it bears repeating: *we like people who like us.*

The secret to genuine charming likability is to find commonalities, similarities, and positive traits between yourself and another party, and then express them. The secret to unleashing your inner charm and likability is to find the value in those around you. The secret is to genuinely like other people—even people that you may find it tough to like.

 Warning: Don't fake it. Don't make stuff up. Sincerely respect and value what you are expressing to the other person. You don't have to be best friends, but you do need to convince others that you are sincerely interested. The surest and easiest way to do that is to actually be interested.

By going through the process of finding genuine value *you* will sincerely like the other person more and they will, in turn, genuinely like you more. This is the commonly overlooked and perhaps under-estimated secret to charm and likability.

Some people may argue, "Why bother being charming? Being liked by your clients, your boss, or your coworkers should have absolutely no bearing on performance or achievement." The problem is that if your target market doesn't like you, they won't hire you; if your potential boss doesn't like you, you won't get hired to begin with; and if your coworkers don't like you, they have no incentive to help you.

Charming likability is often an overlooked secret to success.

The Myth of Charisma

Whether you call it charm or charisma, the person who possesses this quality is powerful. They have a knack for making their conversation partner feel like the most important person in the room. Most people think of charisma and charm as intangible qualities, irreducible character traits, an "X-factor" that only a select few are born with.

However, that's a myth!

Research[2,3,4] suggests that charisma is a set of behaviors, or internal characteristics, that can be developed. Even the shyest people can transform themselves into charismatic charmers. And that's great news, because that means it's inside all of us, and we can all learn to unlock our charismatic potential. We all can be the person everyone else is attracted to, is charmed by, and enjoys conversing with. It means that being charismatic and likable is, in fact, a choice.

Warning: Being charming and charismatic doesn't mean sucking up, being extroverted, bubbly, or witty.

According to Olivia Fox Cabane, author of *The Charisma Myth,* having charisma means demonstrating presence, warmth, and power all the same time. For me, it means showing genuine care for others, while at the same time exuding authentic authority.

Increase Positive Moments

But before we talk about how you can develop these skills, allow me a small, but important, digression about the importance of positive moments. Dr. Daniel Kahnemen, one of the world's most influential psychologists specializing in how our experiences affect our abilities and perceptions, suggests[5] that we experience approximately 20,000 moments each day and the quality of our day is determined by how our brains recognize and interpret these moments. He describes three general classifications of moments that our brains track: positive, negative, and neutral. Kahneman says our mood is defined by the ratio of positive to negative experiences over the course of a day.

Quick Quiz: Do you think you experience more positive moments than negative moments? What do you think your personal average positive to negative ratio is? How about your work environment? What is the ratio there?

Researchers have spent a lot of time exploring how the ratio of positive to negative experiences affects both our work and personal lives. Remember, in chapter 6 on delivering feedback, I mentioned how the magic ratio of 5:1 was used to predict marital success.

In the workplace, psychologist Marcial Losada showed[6] that you need at least a positivity/negativity ratio of approximately 3:1 and maximum of 11:1 for teams to flourish. That means you should aim for at least three (and a maximum of eleven) positive interactions for every one negative interaction. In this "Losada Zone" teams report that time flies by, creativity thrives, and productivity increases dramatically. Below that ratio teams become incapable of working together effectively. In fact, Losada reported that in one organization the initial ratio was raised from 1.5:1 to 3.5:1 and the productivity increased by 40 percent.

Psychologist Sidney Jourard found[7] that a staggering 85 percent of a person's happiness in life comes not from possessions, accomplishments, or achievements, but from positive interactions with other people.

Here's another important point: people are attracted to positive people. So in order to attract others to us we need to be positive and genuinely happy ourselves. The good news is that according to psychologists, happiness is also a choice[8]. Interestingly, research also suggests[9] that happiness comes down to having meaningful connections (sound familiar?). In fact, according to actionforhappiness.org, "the main external factor affecting a person's happiness is the quality of their relationships, at home, at work, and in the community."

When taken together, all this data suggests major implications for how we can improve the quality of our lives and how we might go about unleashing our inner charm. The key is to leave people feeling good about their encounters with you. It's about creating positive moments for others (which in turn creates positive moments for yourself).

Quick Quiz: What have you done or said to others today? In what ways do you think you could improve the positive to negative ratio of those around you?

The next step is to make sure you're on the winning side of someone's positive-to-negative ratio. Here are some ways to positively influence people's perceptions of you and increase your likability and charm so you can maximize the positive moments in your life.

Be Yourself

One of my favorite quotes from Oscar Wilde is, "Be yourself; everyone else is taken." In order to unleash our inner charm, we need to first accept ourselves *as we are*. There's no need to wish you were someone else, or to try to be like somebody else. This is important not only for yourself, but also for others around you. No one else will be comfortable with you until you can first be comfortable with yourself.

Of course, this is much easier said than done. We sometimes find ourselves constrained by our environment. We feel as though we can't be ourselves. "What if others don't like me? What if they think I'm [insert your own fear here]? What if they find out that I'm not who they think I am?" However unleashing your inner charm requires you to take the risk, speak from your heart, and radiate who you really are. As Ralph Waldo Emerson wisely said, "Make the most of yourself, for that is all there is of you."

One way to help you understand and become more comfortable in who you are is to ask three people you know through work, three in your personal life, and three in your family what they view as your unique talent. You might consider using the classic tool used by cognitive psychologists called the Johari Window[10] as a springboard for this exercise (you can find an online version at kevan.org/johari).

Choose people who know you well and are trustworthy. Your answers may be surprising and can help you to discover or reinforce your own unique voice.

Respect Others

You then can use this self-confidence to accept others for who they are. You probably don't want anyone changing you; so don't try to change anyone else.

Genuinely respecting yourself and others is the foundation of charm and charisma.

No doubt, you've heard of the Golden Rule: "Do unto others as you would have them do unto you." When it comes to charm, though, remember that it's all about the other person. The truth of the matter is that people and organizations act within their own self-interests. Because of this, you should instead remember to practice the Platinum Rule: "Do unto others as *they* would have you do unto *them*." In short, treat other people the way *they* want to be treated.

Each and every one of us has the power to change another person's entire day, simply with one single word or sentence. Think about all of those times when you may have been having a rough day until someone showed you an act of kindness or said something really nice and insightful. It probably made you feel a lot better, if only because you knew that someone cared.

Likewise, I'll bet there's been an instance or two when someone was extremely rude or angry with you, for apparently no reason. Even if that person wasn't particularly important to you, you probably stewed about it for hours—all because of a few silly words. Make sure people know you care about how they feel and treat them the way they want to be treated.

Finally, the deepest form of respect is empathy. It could be as simple as hearing someone sigh and you respond by saying, "Sounds like you're having a tough day. Anything I can do to help?" or trying to resolve a conflict when a boss says to an employee, "I respect how you're feeling overwhelmed. Let's try to work it out." By expressing empathy to others, they feel like they are being heard.

There's a lot that people don't get to talk about during their day because of time and work constraints. When you give someone the space to be heard—unconditionally—you increase your likability and charm.

 Warning: It's also important to set limits. It's one thing to be empathetic, but it's another to be dumped on. If someone is simply in "poor me" complaining mode, it's reasonable to limit your interactions. Here's a good way to transition out of the whine: "I know you're stressed out. Why don't you take a break and we'll talk when you are ready to discuss possible solutions."

Follow Thumper's Rule and the Magic Ratio

"If you can't say something nice, don't say nothing at all" is a phrase I'm sure you've heard before and is from Disney's classic movie *Bambi*. This advice may sound basic and obvious, however, I see this rule violated on a daily basis. The fact is no one likes to hear someone put another person down. Just like positivity is attractive, negativity is repulsive. Although you would think I wouldn't need to include this in the book, a good rule of thumb is; think twice before expressing negativity. Ask yourself, "What are the consequences of not expressing this?"

Especially in our professional lives there are times when we need to voice dissension or disagreement. It's important, though, to do our best to keep it as positive and constructive as possible. Keep in mind Gottman's Magic Ratio (chapter 6) and aim for five positive comments to every one negative comment. To be perceived as a positive person, pay attention to what people are doing right rather than what's going wrong.

Recognize Strengths

Charismatic leaders show respect by valuing the strengths of the people around them. I sincerely believe that each of us have our own unique value which we bring to our relationships and interactions.

For example, when I hear an intern at lisabmarshall.com say "Oh, I'm just an intern . . ." I make it a point to explain, "Yes, you are an intern, but good interns bring tremendous value to an organization. Interns bring enthusiasm, energy, and fresh eyes. That is difficult, if not impossible, to replicate."

Everyone has strengths. Charismatic leaders consistently recognize and express the strengths of others.

Forgive me for sounding naive, but I also believe that each of us, when in the moment, try to do the best we can. What I mean is that I don't think that most people consciously choose to do wrong. So when I feel wronged or offended, I try very hard to remind myself that I may not know everything that's going on in the other person's life.

Maybe the mom who never volunteers at school is dealing with a sick parent and simply doesn't have the energy to give anymore. Maybe the guy in your office who comes in late, always looks tired, and is sometimes irritable, is suffering from Lupus. Maybe the kid in school who appears aloof lost a parent. I bring up these specific examples because they really were people in my life about whom I had initial misconceptions. I didn't know the root of their outward behavior until I dug deeper which allowed me to connect with them.

Express Appreciation and Gratitude

One way to recognize and highlight strengths is to give others sincere compliments. As Abraham Lincoln said, "Everybody likes a compliment." Let them know what you specifically appreciate in them. Birthdays and holidays are always a good time to explicitly express your gratitude. Take the time to handwrite a heartfelt note that includes small details. At work, reward employees with kind words when they land an important client or complete a huge project. Again, the key is to highlight specific behaviors that you've noticed that you really do value. Everyone enjoys hearing a sincere compliment.

Most people particularly enjoy unexpected compliments or surprise gifts. It's not that they don't appreciate compliments at other times; it just means more when a compliment comes naturally and for no particular reason it will be appreciated more.

For example, if someone says, "This has been such a tough week! My coworker was being a bully and I finally just lost it and told her off! I apologized later, but I still feel terrible." You can help take the edge off their negative feeling by saying something like "Coworkers can be challenging sometimes, but good for you for standing up for yourself. And it's really great that you apologized later. That person is lucky to have a coworker like you!"

 Quick Quiz: Has anyone ever told you that they appreciate the job you do, for no reason other than just to let you know? How did you feel? Did it make you feel as though they sincerely valued you and your contributions?

Express Sincere Flattery

Have you ever heard "Flattery will get you everywhere"? Or maybe you've heard in the opposite form, "Flattery will get you nowhere"? Interestingly, both are true!

It turns out that it's difficult to separate ingratiating compliments from truly kind, flattering compliments. It's human nature to believe them both. According to Robert Cialdini[11], expert on influence and persuasion "praise is the *only* information that is just as successful when it's false as when it's true . . . We *like* people who give us phony compliments *just as much as* people who give us genuine compliments and we believe them equally." Put simply: flattery works.

In fact, a 2010 a research study[12] identified seven effective techniques of subtle flattery that helped executives win board seats. Here is what the authors suggest based on their study:

- Frame flattery as advice: "How were you able to close the deal so successfully?"
- Argue first, then agree: "At first, I didn't see your point, but now I understand. You've convinced me."
- Compliment the manager to friends in his or her network: "I'm learning so much from Roger. He is one of the best managers I've ever worked for."
- Frame flattery as likely to make the manager uncomfortable: "I don't want to embarrass you, but your speech was outstanding. For me it was extremely powerful and inspirational."
- Agree with the manager's values: "I feel the same way. I also believe in XYZ and I agree that we should go forward with the project."
- Agree with manager's opinion after learning it from a third party: "Roger told me what you said at that meeting and I couldn't agree more!"
- Mention common affiliation before flattery: "I watched the national convention last night. What did you think of . . . ?"

In the book, *Power: Why Some People Have It—And Others Don't*, author Jeffrey Pfeffer says[13]:

Most people underestimate the effectiveness of flattery and therefore underutilize it . . . There is simply no question that the desire to believe that flattery is at once sincere and accurate will, in most instances, leave us susceptible to being flattered and, as a consequence, under the influence of the flatterer. So, don't underestimate—or underutilize—the strategy of flattery.

However, keep in mind genuine flattery (otherwise known as praise) is better. Why? First of all, in many instances, the target of blatant, insincere flattery will notice. If your conversation partner senses you're "laying it on" they may discount your words of praise. What's worse, they may resent you for delivering an insincere compliment, which can make the recipient feel used, manipulated, and condescended to.

However, if instead, you give a sincere compliment, your words will have the opposite effect. The person whom you are complimenting will feel uplifted and positively energized. They will feel liked and appreciated. Remember, as I previously mentioned in chapters 2 and 11, because of the powerful concept of reciprocity, people have a strong tendency to like people who like them. Your *sincere* praise will serve to strengthen the relationship.

When you're able to discover something worthy of a genuine compliment, you end up genuinely liking that person more because you have found and expressed a shared value. You will like them, they'll return the affection, which will make you like them even more, and so on ... making your connection tighter and stronger.

In addition, simply for ethical reasons, sincere praise is better. Always being genuine is probably the hardest part of giving compliments (especially when you have little in common with someone), but for me it's important to wait until you've discovered something you can sincerely praise. You don't want to be a sycophant, you want to establish common ground and really get to know the person. *Smart Talk* flattery is sincere and genuine.

How Do You Deliver a Good Compliment?

I often get asked about how to give compliments, especially when the person you want to charm isn't the most popular person in the office. Here's the most effective technique.

Think about the person you want to compliment and concentrate on their personal characteristics that you admire, or can at least respect. Point out something that the person has actually done (or wears) or desires to be. For example, in the story at the beginning of this chapter, the office manager is notoriously stingy. Rather than focusing on her stinginess, though, maybe you can appreciate the work and dedication she puts into her job. You can compliment her on the fact that she is doing her part to keep costs down in a difficult economy.

Second, be specific. Sure, general compliments are nice to hear, but it's far better to let someone know exactly what it is you like about them or their work. This is an excellent way to reinforce positive behaviors. Don't just say "you're a nice person," or "you look nice today." Instead, try saying "I really appreciate the way you smoothly handled that situation with Accounting," or "That's a really great looking sweater." The key is to not leave them guessing about what you mean.

Third, be timely but patient. What do I mean by that? Wait for the right time to give a compliment. Don't try to manufacture the moment, but instead allow the opportunity to present itself. When you try to force the timing of a compliment, you give the appearance that it's all about you; you're complimenting the person when it's right or convenient for you, not them. Remember, in order to effectively unleash your inner charm, you need to put the other person first. Your interactions with them should always be about them.

Lastly, don't say more than you have to. I don't mean that you should shy away from a conversation. But once you've told them what you needed to say, don't keep rambling on about it. Move on to another topic. The longer you dwell on giving a compliment, the more likely it will be that the recipient will begin to doubt your sincerity.

VIP Bonus: Do you have trouble receiving compliments? **VIP** Download "How to Receive a Compliment With Grace" and get other exclusive information and benefits by joining my *free* members-only VIP site at www.smarttalksuccess .com/VIP.

Be Humble

Charming people are also good at accepting compliments with humility and grace. Accepting compliments is an art form that few have mastered. People with charisma make it a point to let the giver know that their compliment is sincerely appreciated, which makes the person giving the compliment feel good about themselves, as well.

Humility extends beyond compliments. Charming people are humble with all their words. No one likes a braggart. It's okay to talk about things that you've accomplished as matters of fact, but don't build yourself up. Let others attach attributes to those activities or request more information about them. No need to shout; warm and friendly works better.

For example, if someone says "Wow, that's an unusual jacket, I've never seen one like it before!" Don't say, "Oh, yes, I attended the Cannes Film Festival with a billionaire friend of mine and afterward we took a train to Monte Carlo and I got this coat in a little boutique near the main casino." Instead, stick with "Oh, thanks. I haven't seen another one locally either." If the other person wants more information about the coat, they'll ask for it.

This lesson applies particularly when participating in online conversations. While it's OK to post your successes and achievements every now and again, they should be lightly sprinkled among many more tips and tricks to help your clients. Again, the key idea is to put others first.

Admit Your Mistakes

Try to view mistakes as experience. Steve Jobs, cofounder of Apple and Pixar, said, "Sometimes when you innovate, you make mistakes. It is best to admit them quickly, and get on with improving your other innovations." Stubbornness and rigidity are definitely unlikable traits. Of course, the best thing is to not do anything you will be sorry for, but that's not realistic.

When you've made a mistake, be quick with a sincere apology. An apology can be as simple as "Yes, you're right. I had that wrong. Thanks for letting me know." Even when the situation is more complicated, if you've made a mistake, recognize the error and openly face whatever consequences may come your way without grumbling. Formal apologies should include: a specific statement of the offense, acknowledgment of the damage that was done, taking responsibility for your actions, a statement of apology, asking for forgiveness and, finally, asking how you can make restitution. This last step is often skipped but I believe is the most powerful and should never be skipped. This shows honesty and integrity, two thoroughly likable and charming qualities.

 Warning: An insincere, unbelievable "I'm sorry" can do more harm than good. Be careful not to apologize too much.

Laugh More

When you've made a mistake, it never hurts to laugh at yourself. When you can share a laugh or a smile with someone, it makes others more receptive to you. Especially when we are not afraid to laugh at ourselves, we'll be perceived as mature, balanced, and trustworthy. You will be perceived as more attractive.

Many studies have confirmed the value of smiling and humor.[14, 15] Laughter reduces tension,[16] it helps people reach agreement, and it increases attraction, all of which are charming characteristics. In addition, smiling faces are easier to remember.

One study[17] showed that smiling promotes trust among strangers. One of the study's coauthors, Rick Wilson, said in an interview,[18] "People who have friendly expressions are rated better or perceived to be nicer. Our study shows that people not only make those attributions, but they will even rely on them when there are financial risks." Another study[19] found that looking at an attractive face activates regions of the brain associated with drug addiction. It's like a natural high. And if the face is smiling, the brain lights up even more[20].

One really interesting study[21] found that when mothers viewed their baby's smiling faces, this also activated the same regions of the brain. That certainly explains the feeling I get when I look at the baby picture of my twin girls that I keep in my wallet. If possible, I sneak a peek at their photos just before I am about to meet new people. Sometimes I just visualize the image in my head. It immediately brings a smile to my face and I feel warm. People have told me they can see the warmth in my face. I also use this same visualization after I've had a negative interaction because it can really positively alter my mood. I recommend that everyone have a photo on their cell phone and in their wallet just for this purpose. And it doesn't have to be of children, at all. You can visualize any person, a pet, or even a higher power who is important to you. Choose whatever makes you glow with warmth and affection.

Remember the Details

Quite often, people we think are charming demonstrate a remarkable ability to recall details. Make it a point to record and review the details of those around you. I had a boss once—a CEO, actually, far above my pay grade at the time—who remembered some of the most obscure aspects about the people he met. His ability to recall specific details made people believe that he genuinely cared about them and wanted them to succeed. You really felt as if he knew you when he spoke to you, even if you had never had a conversation with him before. Needless to say, he was a very popular leader, and people flocked to him.

Get Close

Finally, charming people recognize and take advantage of proximity. E-mailing or texting someone is one thing, but meeting someone in person changes things immensely. There is a significant intangible benefit from meeting in person. In fact, according to social psychologists[22], we are more likely to develop a relationship with someone who is in close physical proximity. Basically, it's easier to talk with someone sitting next to you than with someone across the room.

I probably shouldn't admit this, but when I was in college, on the first day of class, I used to wait in the back of the room until it was about two-thirds full. Then I would choose the guy I found most attractive and sit near him. This strategy worked so well that I still use a similar strategy at conferences—*except,* of course, now my goal is to build and strengthen business relationships.

Whether it's the boardroom, a conference room, or a classroom, take advantage of the space by always strategically choosing who you want to be physically close to. Especially today when so much work is done online, remember that meeting people in person is extremely important, particularly when it comes to perceptions of charisma.

I hope you have been doing the chapter quizzes up to this point, but if not, this is definitely a chapter that requires you to dive in and practice. Deep down inside, you are a charismatic charmer—and you can learn how to bring your charm to the surface more often. All it takes is practice, starting with the chapter quizzes. I'd like to strongly encourage you to try the challenges at the end of this chapter and get out there and wow the world with your new charming, charismatic self!

Summary: How to Unleash Your Inner Charisma

✓ Having charisma or charm means demonstrating presence, warmth, and power all at the same time.
✓ Research suggests that charisma is a set of behaviors, or internal characteristics, that can be developed, not an inherent "you either have it, or you don't" quality.

✓ The secret to genuine charisma is to find commonalities, similarities, and positive traits that you sincerely admire in others and express them.

✓ Charisma and charm is about creating positive moments for others and for yourself.

✓ Genuine respect for yourself and others is the foundation of charm and charisma.

✓ Charming people focus on the positive, even when voicing disagreement.

✓ Charismatic leaders show respect by valuing the strengths of the people around them.

✓ Charismatic leaders express appreciation through compliments and sincere flattery.

✓ Steps to delivering a compliment:

1. Concentrate on personal characteristics that you admire or respect.

2. Be as specific as possible.

3. Be timely by waiting for the right moment to deliver the compliment.

4. Be brief.

✓ Charming people show humility through gracious acceptance of compliments, by admitting mistakes, and offering quick, sincere apologies.

✓ Charismatic people readily share genuine smiles and enjoy humor.

✓ Charming people remember details and understand the importance of close proximity.

Smart Talk Challenge #1

List five people you admire across many industries. List 3–5 characteristics that you admire about them. For example: integrity, collaborative leadership, tireless work ethic, commitment to community, etc. Look for commonalities or patterns. Choose the two characteristics that are most important to you then make the statement, "I am committed to X." Write it down and repeat the phrase to others in natural conversation throughout the next two weeks. This alone will bring about changes.

Smart Talk Challenge #2

Think about the three main elements of charm: putting others first, showing genuine care for others, and exuding authentic authority. Honestly rank your abilities and skills in each area. Create three concrete steps you can take to become stronger in your weakest area. They don't have to be big things, just little steps that will move you in the right direction. For example, if putting others first is the characteristic you chose, you might write:

1. When someone interacts with me, stop doing whatever I am doing and turn my body so that I am facing them directly.
2. Make direct eye contact during our conversation.
3. When I greet someone, be first to ask about something that is important to them.
4. When my mind wanders, notice, and bring myself quickly back to the conversation by focusing.

Smart Talk Challenge #3

For one day, track how many sincere compliments you give to other people. The next day, try to improve that number by 25 percent. Choose people you see often and make it a point to thank them for their efforts. Tell them how you appreciate what they do. Consider experimenting with three of the seven strategies for subtle flattery. Remember to always be sincere with your compliments.

Case Study: Deborah Spivack, Member of the American Academy of Adoption Attorneys

"Earlier in my career, while trying to establish myself as an attorney, I realized I needed to project a professional public image for court appearances, speaking opportunities, and client development. It was difficult because I was reserved and soft spoken. I also lacked confidence in the subject matter since I was inexperienced.

"My stumbling blocks were that I did not feel comfortable becoming the type of professional person I saw around me. Other women attorneys appeared to have a very different style from mine and I could not, and did not want to, emulate them. I simply did not know how my personality could fit into a professional and public role without becoming an entirely different person. I also lacked passion for the work I was doing at the time.

"The first major step I took to address this issue was to find a public role model, a person who projected herself in the manner that I believed could match my own style in a positive way. I realized that all people do not need to project the same image to be viewed as professional, competent, and capable. Rather, we can utilize our own strengths to project our personal qualities in a way that feels genuine. This realization was a huge breakthrough for me.

"Seeing someone who possessed similar personality traits and style leverage her strengths and succeed showed me that I could accomplish my professional needs without changing my core personality. Second, I realized that my lack of confidence was due to a lack of passion for the subject matter in which I practiced. Although I was an attorney, I realized that I did not want to be limited by my professional training, but rather, to find my passion and build a career around that. I even considered leaving the practice of law altogether.

"When I took the time to consider who I had admired most in the world (not within just the practice of law), I recalled a story I had seen on television about a woman, Betty Tisdale, who had rescued many orphans shortly after the Vietnam War by finding them families with Americans who wanted to be parents. I researched her to learn more.

"I realized I admired her role in helping children who did not have families come together with families who wanted to be parents. I also admired her determination to fight for these children using assertiveness, creativity, and tenaciousness. Finally, I admired her decision to pursue goals that were not common among her peers or popular generally. She followed her heart without considering how it was different than others around her.

"Betty's experience and accomplishments inspired me to take steps to change my life.

"I contacted her and volunteered with some of her local contacts. I then took a new job outside of the field of law and a big salary reduction to learn about adoption. I also used my law degree to advocate for regulatory changes and became thoroughly familiar with areas of the international laws governing adoption. Finally, I started my own law practice in adoption, a field for which I am extremely passionate.

"It felt wonderful to finally enjoy the subject matter I was working in, and the professional opportunities related to it. I became a voracious reader of all materials that increased my knowledge in my new field, and due to my deep understanding of it, I automatically projected more confidence.

"Once entrenched in my new practice area, I found dozens of people who I admire and relate to among my colleagues. My client cases each feel very personal and I want to do my very best work on their behalf. I found a career in the law that I simply love and grew naturally into the type of professional person I needed to be to succeed.

"I feel confident and enthusiastic about my career and welcome opportunities for speaking, meeting with clients, and court appearances. Clients and colleagues seem to appreciate that I have a passion for my work and that my wish to help them achieve their goals is genuine and important to me."

Conclusion:
Smart Talk—The X-Factor of Success

Smart talk, as we have seen in each chapter of this book, is one of the most effective ways to influence others and to get the most fulfillment out of work and life. Smart talk is the X-factor of success.

Becoming a master smart talker is a slow and steady process, not a competition or sprint. Harnessing the power of *Smart Talk* communication means making people feel good about themselves, so that they feel good about you. It means listening to people and letting them know you care.

Becoming a master of smart talk will give you influence over your coworkers, employees, friends, and family. And, as with all power, possessing smart talk communication skills brings with it a great responsibility.

As you practice and experience the profound ways in which you can develop and strengthen your communication skills, you'll experience an increase in your personal power. If you use this power with positive intent for others, you will be acting from an inner platform of integrity that will serve to electrify your life and bring you to your next level, whatever that may be.

When you are able to unleash inner power, you truly do make

your environment better. You can become a positive influence in the workplace and in the home. Effective communicators get what they need and want, when they need and want it, without steam-rolling others to get it.

Smart talkers command respect because they give respect, and as a result they wield influence.

This is not the end. It's just the beginning.

Psssst . . . Don't forget to visit www.smarttalksuccess.com/ quiz and retake the Smart Talk quiz. Also, I'd like to personally invite you to join my social networks. As always, you can send your questions and feedback to me at lisa@lisabmarshall.com.

Endnotes

Introduction: The (Not So) Hidden Cost of Saying the Wrong Thing

1. "SMB Communications Pain Study White Paper: Uncovering the hidden cost of communications barriers and latency," SIS International Research, accessed April 2, 2012, http://www.marketintelligences.com/industrial -b2b-journal/2009/3/10/smb-communications-pain-study-white-paper -uncovering-the-hid.html.

2. *Communication Success: Tips for Busy People,* HP ePrintCenter, accessed April 2, 2012, https://h30495.www3.hp.com/detail/1237.2.

1. Taking the "Hell" Out of Hello: How to Introduce Yourself

1. Daniel Goleman, *Emotional Intelligence* (Bantam Dell Pub Group, 1996), 18–20.

2. Michael Sunnafrank and Artemio Ramirez, "At First Sight: Persistent Relational Effects of Get-Acquainted Conversations," *Journal of Social and Personal Relationships,* 21 (2004): 361–379.

3. "How is Handshaking Related to Personality?," Brad Bell, accessed April 2, 2012, http://www.psychologyandsociety.com/handshaking.html.

4. Wikipedia contributors, "Handshake," Wikipedia, The Free Encyclopedia, http://en.wikipedia.org/wiki/Handshake (accessed April 2, 2012).

5. Guy Kawasaki, *Enchantment: The Art of Changing Hearts, Minds, and Actions* (New York: Penguin, 2011), 44.

6. Jeffrey Gitomer, *Little Black Book of Connections: 6.5 Assets for Networking Your Way to Rich Relationships* (Austin: Bard Press, 2006), 144.

7. Tim Sanders, *Love Is the Killer App: How to Win Business and Influence Friends* (New York: Crown Business, 2003), 119.

2. Conversation Magic: How to Improve Your Conversation Skills

1. "10-Foot Rule," Walmart Stores, Inc., accessed April 2, 2012, http://walmartstores.com/AboutUs/285.aspx.

2. Julia Wood, *Interpersonal communication: Everyday encounters* (5th ed.). (Cengage Learning Products, 2010).

3. Paul C. Cozby, "Self-Disclosure: A literature review," *Psychological Bulletin*, 79(2)(1973): 151–160.

4. Kathryn Dindia and Mike Allen, "Sex differences in self-disclosure: A meta-analysis, *Psychological Bulletin*, 112(1)(1992): 106–124.

5. Kathryn Green, et al., "Self-Disclosure in Personal Relationships," in *The Cambridge Handbook of Personal Relationships*, ed. Anita L. Vangelisti et al. (Cambridge University Press, 2006), 409.

6. Green, *The Cambridge Handbook of Personal Relationships*, 412–446.

7. Nancy L. Collins and Lynn Carol Miller, "Self-disclosure and liking: A meta-analytic review," *Psychological Bulletin*, 116(3)(1994): 457–475.

3. Cat Got Your Tongue? What to Say When ...

1. Meghan Casserly, December 2, 2010, "True Stories From The Holiday Party Files," *Forbes Blog*, http://www.forbes.com/sites/meghancasserly/2010/12/02/holiday-office-party-bad-behavior/.

4. Giddyup Your Follow-Up: How to Effectively Follow Up on Your Conversations

1. Jay Conrad Levinson, *Guerilla Marketing Attack*, (MA: Houghton Mifflin Company, 1989).

5. From Archie Bunker to Mary Poppins: How to Speak with Tact and Grace

1. Robert Bolton and Dorothy Grover Bolton, *People Styles at Work: Making Bad Relationships Good and Good Relationships Better*, (New York: AMACOM, 1996).

2. Wikipedia contributors, "DISC assessment," Wikipedia, The Free Encyclopedia, http://en.wikipedia.org/wiki/DISC_assessment (accessed April 4, 2012).

3. Wikipedia contributors, "Keirsey Temperament Sorter," Wikipedia, The Free Encyclopedia, http://en.wikipedia.org/wiki/Keirsey_Temperament _Sorter (accessed April 4, 2012).

6. Fearless Feedback: How to Deliver Restorative Feedback

1. Marcial Losada, "The complex dynamics of high-performance teams," *Mathematical and Computer Modeling* 30(1999): 179–192.

2. John M. Gottman, et.al. "Predicting marital happiness and stability from newlywed interactions," *Journal of Marriage and the Family* 60(1)(1998): 5–22.

3. John M. Gottman and Robert W. Levenson, "A Two-Factor Model for Predicting When a Couple Will Divorce: Exploratory Analyses Using 14-Year Longitudinal Data," *Family Process* 41(1)(2002): 83–96.

4. Sybil Carrère, et.al. "Predicting Marital Stability and Divorce in Newlywed Couples," *Journal of Family Psychology* 14(1)(2000): 42–58.

5. Gerald B. Hickson, et.al., "A Complementary Approach to Promoting Professionalism: Identifying, Measuring, and Addressing Unprofessional Behaviors," *Academic Medicine* 82(11)(2007): 142–145.

6. Adam Bryant, "At Yum Brands, Rewards for Good Work," *New York Times,* (2009), accessed June 11, 2012, http://www.nytimes.com/2009/07 /12/bussines/12corner.html?_r=1.

8. We Have to Talk: How to Have a Difficult Conversation

1. Kenneth W. Thomas and Ralph H. Kilmann, *Thomas-Kilmann Conflict Mode Instrument* (New York: XICOM, 1974).

2. Alison L. Hill, et. al., "Emotions as infectious diseases in a large social network: the SISa model," *Proceedings of the Royal Society—B,* (2010), accessed April 7, 2012, http://rspb.royalsocietypublishing.org/content/277 /1701/3827.

11. The Art (and Science) of Persuasion: How to Influence Others

1. Robert B. Cialdini, *Influence: The Psychology of Persuasion* (New York: Collins, 2007).

2. Melissa Allison, "Retiring CEO of Costco takes a look back on his legacy," *Seattle Times,* (2011), accessed April 7, 2012, http://seattletimes.nwsource .com/html/businesstechnology/2017040471_sinegal18.html.

3. Jonathan L. Freedman and Scott C. Fraser, "Compliance without pressure: The foot-in-the-door technique," *Journal of Personality and Social Psychology* 4(1966): 195–202.

4. Jerry. M. Burger, "The foot-in-the-door compliance procedure: A multiple-process analysis and review," *Personality and Social Psychology Review* 3(1999): 303–325.

5. James P. Dillard, "Self-inference and the foot-in-the-door technique: Quantity of behavior and attitudinal mediation," *Human Communication Research* 16(1990): 422–447.

6. Jerry M. Burger et al., "The Effect of Fleeting Attraction on Compliance Requests," *Personality and Social Psychology Bulletin* 27(12)(2001): 1578–1586, accessed April 7, 2012, doi: 10.1177/01461672012712002.

7. Ellen J. Langer, *Mindfulness* (MA: Addison-Wesley, 1989).

8. Jennifer E. Escalas, "Narrative versus Analytical Self-Referencing and Persuasion," *Journal of Consumer Research* 34(4)(2007): 421–429.

9. Melanie C. Green, "Transportation into narrative worlds: The role of prior knowledge and perceived realism," *Discourse Processes* 38(2004): 247–266.

10. "Principle 6 Liking part 2—Ciadini," YouTube video, 7:33, from a lecture on the science of influence at CalTech in 2011, posted by "newage-science," October 10, 2011, http://www.youtube.com/watch?v=hXpysRR eBmk&feature=relmfu.

12. The Art of the Deal: How to Negotiate

1. Pat Croce, "Do Your Homework." Eye on Entrepreneur (blog), accessed April 7, 2012, http://www.patcroce.com/entrepreneur/homework.html.

2. Alex Crippen, "CNBC Transcript: Warren Buffett's $200B Berkshire Blunder and the Valuable Lesson He Learned." CNBC Warren Buffet Watch (blog), access April 8, 2013, http://www.cnbc.com/id/39724884/CNBC_Tran script_Warren_Buffett_s_200B_Berkshire_Blunder_and_the_Valuable _Lesson_He_Learned.

14. Magically Delicious: How to Unleash Your Inner Charisma

1. Carlin Flora, "The X-Factors of Success," Psychology Today Blog, last modified December 28, 2011, http://www.psychologytoday.com/articles /200505/the-x-factors-success.

2. Robert J. House, "A 1976 theory of charismatic leadership," in *Leadership: The Cutting Edge*, ed. James G. Hunt and Lars Larson, (Carbondale: Southern Illinois University Press, 1977), 189–207.

3. Robert J. House, and M. Baetz, "Leadership: Some empirical generalizations and new research directions," in *Research in Organizational Behavior*, ed. B. M. Staw (Greenwich, CT: JAI Press, 1979) 1: 341–423.

4. Robert J. House and Jane M. Howell, "Personality and charismatic leadership," in *Leadership Quarterly* 3(1992): 81–108.

5. Daniel Kahneman and Jason Riis, "Living and Thinking about It: Two Perspectives on Life," in *The Science of Well-Being* (Oxford University Press, 2005), 285–301.

6. Marcial Losada and Emily Heaphy, "The role of positivity and connectivity in the performance of business teams: A nonlinear dynamics model," *American Behavioral Scientist*, 47 (6)(2004): 740–765. doi: 10.1177 /0002764203260208.

7. Sidney M. Jourard, *Self-disclosure: An Experimental Analysis of the Transparent Self* (New York: Wiley, 1971).

8. Wikipedia contributors, "Happiness," Wikipedia, The Free Encyclopedia, http://en.wikipedia.org/wiki/Happiness (accessed April 2, 2012).

9. Ed Diener and Martin EP. Seligman, "Very Happy," *Psychological Science* 13 (2002): 81–84.

10. Wikipedia contributors, "Johari window," Wikipedia, The Free Encyclopedia, http://en.wikipedia.org/wiki/Johari_window (accessed April 19, 2012).

11. "Principle 6 liking part 1 Ciadini," YouTube video, 10:10, from a lecture on the science of influence at CalTech in 2011, posted by "newagescience," October 10, 2011, http://www.youtube.com/watch?v=ftr48APX0UM.

12. Ithai Stern and James D. Westphal, "Stealthy Footsteps to the Boardroom: Executives' Backgrounds, Sophisticated Interpersonal Influence Behavior, and Board Appointments" in *Administrative Science Quarterly* 55(2010): 278–319.

13. Jeffrey Pfeffer, *Power: Why Some People Have It—And Others Don't*, (New York: HarperCollins Publishers, 2010), 34.

14. Mary Payne Bennet and Celile Lengacher, "Humor and Laughter May Influence Health: III. Laughter and Health Outcomes" in *Evidence Based Complementary and Alternative Medicine* 5(1) (2008): 37–40. doi: 10.1093 /ecam/nem041.

15. Elizabeth Scott, "The Stress Management and Health Benefits of Laughter" last modified January 10, 2011, http://stress.about.com/od/stresshealth /a/laughter.htm.

16. Mary Payne Bennet, et al., "The Effect of Mirthful Laughter on Stress and Natural Killer Cell Activity" in *Alternative Therapies in Health and Medicine* 9(2)(2003): 38–45.

17. Jörn P.W. Scharlemann, et al., "The value of a smile: Game theory with a human face" in *Journal of Economic Psychology* 22(5) (2001): 617–640.

18. B.J. Almond, "Show Your Pearly Whites," *Sallyport: The Magazine of Rice University*, accessed April 11, 2012, http://www.rice.edu/sallyport/2002/spring/sallyport/pearlywhites.html.

19. Itzhak Aharon, et al., "Beautiful Faces Have Variable Reward Value: fMRI and Behavioral Evidence," in *Neuron* 32(3) (2001): 537–551.

20. John O'Doherty, et al., "Beauty in a smile: the role of medial orbitofrontal cortex in facial attractiveness," in *Neuropsychologia* 41(2) (2003): 147–155.

21. Lane Strathearn, et al., "What's in a Smile? Maternal Brain Responses to Infant Facial Cues," in *Pediatrics* 122(1) (2008): 40–51.

22. "Lecture 08—Social Psych: Interpersonal attraction," accessed April 8, 2012, http://www.nd.edu/~rwilliam/xsoc530/attraction.html.

Bibliography

Allison, Mellisa. "Retiring CEO of Costco takes a look back on his legacy." *Seattle Times* (2011). Accessed April 7, 2012. http://seattletimes.nwsource.com /html/businesstechnology/2017040471_sinegal18.html.

Almond, B. J. *Sallyport* magazine. "Show Your Pearly Whites." Accessed April 11, 2012. http://www.rice.edu/sallyport/2002/spring/sallyport/pearlywhites .html.

Bell, Brad. "How is Handshaking Related to Personality?" Accessed April 2, 2012. http://www.psychologyandsociety.com/handshaking.html.

Bennet, Mary Payne and Celile Lengacher. "Humor and Laughter May Influence Health: III. Laughter and Health Outcomes." *Evidence Based Complementary and Alternative Medicine* 5(1)(2008): 37–40. Accessed April 8, 2012. doi: 10.1093/ecam/nem041.

Bennet, Mary Payne, Janice M. Zeller, Lisa Rosenberg, Judith McCann. "The Effect of Mirthful Laughter on Stress and Natural Killer Cell Activity." *Alternative Therapies in Health and Medicine* 9(2)(2003): 38–45.

Bolton, Robert and Dorothy Grover Bolton. *People Styles at Work: Making Bad Relationships Good and Good Relationships Better.* New York: AMACOM, 1996.

Bryant, Adam. "At Yum Brands Rewards for Good Work" *New York Times* (2009). Accessed June 11, 2012. http://www.nytimes.com/2009/07/12/busi ness/12corner.html.

Burger, Jerry M., Shelley Soroka, Katrina Gonzago, Emily Murphy, Emily Somervell. "The Effect of Fleeting Attraction on Compliance Requests." *Personality and Social Psychology Bulletin* 27(12)(2001): 1578–1586. Accessed April 7, 2012. doi: 10.1177/01461672012712002.

Burger, Jerry. M. "The foot-in-the-door compliance procedure: A multiple-process analysis and review." *Personality and Social Psychology Review* 3(1999): 303–325.

Carrère, Sybil, Kim T. Buehlman, John M. Gottman, James A. Coan and Lionel Ruckstuhl. "Predicting Marital Stability and Divorce in Newlywed Couples." *Journal of Family Psychology* 14(1)(2000): 42–58.

Casserly, Meghan. December 2, 2010. "True Stories From The Holiday Party Files," *Forbes Blog.* http://www.forbes.com/sites/meghancasserly/2010/12/02/holiday-office-party-bad-behavior/.

Cialdini, Robert B. *Influence: The Psychology of Persuasion.* New York: Collins, 2007.

Collins, Nancy L. and Lynn C. Miller. "Self-disclosure and liking: A meta-analytic review." *Psychological Bulletin* 116(1994): 457–475.

Cozby, Paul C. "Self-Disclosure: A literature review." *Psychological Bulletin* 79(2)(1973): 151–160.

Crippen, Alex. "CNBC Transcript: Warren Buffett's $200B Berkshire Blunder and the Valuable Lesson He Learned." CNBC Warren Buffet Watch (blog). Accessed April 8, 2012. http://www.cnbc.com/id/39724884/CNBC_Transcript_Warren_Buffett_s_200B_Berkshire_Blunder_and_the_Valuable_Lesson_He_Learned.

Croce, Pat. "Do Your Homework." Eye on Entrepreneur (blog). Accessed April 7, 2012. http://www.patcroce.com/entrepreneur/homework.html.

Diener, Ed and Martin EP. Seligman. "Very Happy." *Psychological Science* 13 (2002): 81–84.

Dillard, James. "Self-inference and the foot-in-the-door technique: Quantity of behavior and attitudinal mediation." *Human Communication Research* 16(1990): 422–447.

Dindia, Kathryn and Mike Allen. "Sex differences in self-disclosure: A meta-analysis." *Psychological Bulletin* 112(1)(1992): 106–124.

Escalas, Jennifer E. "Narrative versus Analytical Self-Referencing and Persuasion." *Journal of Consumer Research* 34(4)(2007): 421–429.

Flora, Carlin "The X-Factors of Success." Psychology Today Blog. Last modified December 28, 2011. http://www.psychologytoday.com/articles/200505/the-x-factors-success.

Freedman, Jonathan L. and Scott C. Fraser. "Compliance without pressure: The foot-in-the-door technique." *Journal of Personality and Social Psychology* 4(1966): 195–202.

Gitomer, Jeffrey. *Little Black Book of Connections: 6.5 Assets for Networking Your Way to Rich Relationships.* Austin: Bard Press, 2006.

Goleman, Daniel. *Emotional Intelligence.* New York: Bantam Dell Pub Group, 1996.

Gottman, John M. and Robert W. Levenson. "A Two-Factor Model for Predicting When a Couple Will Divorce: Exploratory Analyses Using 14-Year Longitudinal Data." *Family Process* 41 (1)(2002): 83–96.

Green, Kathryn, Valerian J. Derlega and Alicia Mathews. "Self-Disclosure in Personal Relationships." In *The Cambridge Handbook of Personal Relationships,* edited by Anita L. Vangelisti and Daniel Perlman, 409–446. New York: Cambridge University Press, 2006.

Green, Melanie C. "Transportation into narrative worlds: The role of prior knowledge and perceived realism." *Discourse Processes* 38(2004): 247–266.

Hickson, Gerald B., James W. Pichert, Lynn E. Webb and Steven G. Gabbe. "A Complementary Approach to Promoting Professionalism: Identifying, Measuring, and Addressing Unprofessional Behaviors." *Academic Medicine* 82(11)(2007): 142–145.

House, Robert J. and Jane M. Howell. "Personality and charismatic leadership." *Leadership Quarterly* 3(1992): 81–108.

House, Robert J. and M. Baetz, "Leadership: Some empirical generalizations and new research directions." In *Research in Organizational Behavior,* edited by B. M. Staw, 1: 341–423. Greenwich, CT: JAI Press, 1979.

Jourard, Sidney M. *Self-disclosure: An Experimental Analysis of the Transparent Self.* New York: Wiley, 1971.

Kahneman, Daniel and Jason Riis. "Living and Thinking about It: Two Perspectives on Life." In *The Science of Well-Being.* Oxford University Press, 2005: 285–301.

Kawasaki, Guy. *Enchantment: The Art of Changing Hearts, Minds, and Actions.* New York: Penguin, 2011.

Langer, Ellen J. *Mindfulness.* MA: Addison-Wesley, 1989.

"Lecture 08—Social Psych: Interpersonal attraction." Accessed April 8, 2012. http://www.nd.edu/~rwilliam/xsoc530/attraction.html.

Levinson, Jay Conrad. *Guerilla Marketing Attack.* Massachusetts: Houghton Mifflin Company, 1989.

Losada, Marcial and Emily Heaphy. "The role of positivity and connectivity in the performance of business teams: A nonlinear dynamics model." *American Behavioral Scientist,* 47 (6)(2004): 740–765. doi: 10.1177/0002764203260208.

Losada, Marcial. "The complex dynamics of high-performance teams." *Mathematical and Computer Modeling* 30(1999): 179–192.

"Principle 6 Liking part 2—Ciadini." YouTube video, 7:33, from a lecture on the science of influence at CalTech in 2011. Posted by "newagescience." October 10, 2011. http://www.youtube.com/watch?v=hXpysRReBmk&feature=relmfu.

Sanders, Tim, Love Is the Killer App, New York: Three Rivers Press, 2002.

Scharlemann, Jörn P.W., Catherine C Eckel, Alex Kacelnik, Rick K Wilson. *Journal of Economic Psychology* 22(5)(2001): 617–640.

Scott, Elizabeth. "The Stress Management and Health Benefits of Laughter." Accessed April 11, 2012. http://stress.about.com/od/stresshealth/a/laughter.htm.

SIS International Research. "SMB Communications Pain Study White Paper: Uncovering the hidden cost of communications barriers and latency." Accessed April 2, 2012. http://www.marketintelligences.com/industrial-b2b-journal/2009/3/10/smb-communications-pain-study-white-paper-uncovering-the-hid.html.

Sunnafrank, Michael and Artemio Ramirez. "At First Sight: Persistent Relational Effects of Get-Acquainted Conversations." *Journal of Social and Personal Relationships* 21(2004): 361–379.

Thomas, Kenneth W. and Ralph H. Kilmann. *Thomas-Kilmann Conflict Mode Instrument.* Tuxedo, NY: XICOM, 1974.

Walmart Stores, Inc. "10-Foot Rule." Accessed April 2, 2012. http://walmartstores.com/AboutUs/285.aspx.

Wood, Julia T. *Interpersonal Communication: Everyday Encounters.* (6th ed.). CA: Cengage Learning products, 2010.

Index